# SpringerBriefs in Computer Science

SpringerBriefs present concise summaries of cutting-edge research and practical applications across a wide spectrum of fields. Featuring compact volumes of 50 to 125 pages, the series covers a range of content from professional to academic.

Typical topics might include:

- A timely report of state-of-the art analytical techniques
- A bridge between new research results, as published in journal articles, and a contextual literature review
- A snapshot of a hot or emerging topic
- An in-depth case study or clinical example
- A presentation of core concepts that students must understand in order to make independent contributions

Briefs allow authors to present their ideas and readers to absorb them with minimal time investment. Briefs will be published as part of Springer's eBook collection, with millions of users worldwide. In addition, Briefs will be available for individual print and electronic purchase. Briefs are characterized by fast, global electronic dissemination, standard publishing contracts, easy-to-use manuscript preparation and formatting guidelines, and expedited production schedules. We aim for publication 8–12 weeks after acceptance. Both solicited and unsolicited manuscripts are considered for publication in this series.

More information about this series at http://www.springer.com/series/10028

Xin Wei • Liang Zhou

# Multimedia QoE Evaluation

Xin Wei
Liang Zhou

Nanjing University of Posts and Telecommunications
Nanjing, China

ISSN 2191-5768 ISSN 2191-5776 (electronic)
SpringerBriefs in Computer Science
ISBN 978-3-030-23349-5 ISBN 978-3-030-23350-1 (eBook)
https://doi.org/10.1007/978-3-030-23350-1

This Springer imprint is published by the registered company Springer Nature Switzerland AG.
The registered company address is: Gewerbestrasse 11, 6330 Cham, Switzerland

# Preface

With the rapid development of information technology and the establishment of "human-oriented" new type communication fashion, multimedia services have become more and more accessible everywhere, and everyone can quickly obtain the required information from operators or content providers through multimedia terminals. However, future multimedia service emphasizes not only speed, bandwidth, and quality of service sources but also user feeling and satisfaction. Therefore, for multimedia content providers and network operators, promoting user feeling or even their viscosity is very important in the context of video service explosion and heavy competition.

Based on this background, the concept of multimedia quality of experience (QoE), which is a key metric for the description and evaluation of user subjective feeling for multimedia services, receives much attention. However, due to the existence of big data and subjective characteristic of multimedia user experience, there are several pain points and technical challenges during multimedia QoE evaluation. To handle these issues, this book aims at deeply investigating the key technologies and realizations of multimedia QoE evaluation.

In Chap. 1, we provide the background, motivation, and necessity for research on multimedia QoE evaluation. In Chap. 2, we give technical premise and an overview of existing research works on this topic, including the definition of multimedia QoE, various factors influencing QoE, and multimedia QoE evaluation based on machine learning. In Chap. 3, we describe several representative datasets adopted in our research. Moreover, we propose several methods for extracting influencing factors, especially subjective user-related factors such as viewing time ratio, user interest, user type, user behavior, user comment, and danmaku. In Chap. 4, we design several modeling and prediction algorithms, such as multimedia user complaint prediction for imbalanced dataset and multimedia QoE modeling and prediction based on neural networks and broad learning systems. In Chap. 5, based on the theoretical research results, we realize multimedia QoE evaluation based on a big data platform. It concerns data management, data collection and storage, data analysis and mining, and evaluation result demonstration. In Chap. 6, we summarize this book and highlight the future research directions.

The authors would like to thank Prof. Xuemin Sherman Shen of the University of Waterloo for his invitation and valuable suggestions on this book. The authors would also like to thank Ruochen Huang, Yun Gao, Qi Duan, Jiali Mao, Chaoping Lv, and Qifeng Liu of Nanjing University of Posts and Telecommunications for their contributions in the presented research works.

Nanjing, China                                                                          Xin Wei
Nanjing, China                                                                       Liang Zhou
May 2019

# Acknowledgments

This work is partly supported by the National Natural Science Foundation of China (Grant No. 61571240), the Priority Academic Program Development of Jiangsu Higher Education Institutions, and the Natural Science Foundation of Jiangsu Province (Grant No. BK20161517).

# Contents

# Chapter 1
# Introduction

**Abstract** With the rapid development of information technology and the establishment of "human-oriented" new type communication fashion, future multimedia service emphasizes not only speed, bandwidth, quality of service sources, but also user feeling and satisfaction. Therefore, for multimedia content providers and network operators, promoting users' feeling or even their viscosity is very important in the context of multimedia service explosion and heavy competition. In other words, only by continuously improving the recognition and viscosity of users, positioning network services and operational activities into the most valuable user groups, service providers and network operators can achieve the optimization of resource allocation and continuous growth of industry revenue in the fierce competition. Traditional time-consuming and power-intensive user scoring methods can no longer satisfy the multimedia content provider and network operator's evaluation of user satisfaction. Instead, multimedia users' quality of experience (QoE) is evaluated by using the collected big data. Therefore, how to objectively and effectively evaluate multimedia user QoE by considering various influencing factors has become a hot and difficult topic in current research.

## 1.1 Background

In recent years, with the development of Internet technology, multimedia services have become more and more accessible everywhere, and everyone can quickly obtain the required information from operators or content providers through multimedia terminals. According to the statistical data from the Ministry of Industry and Information Technology of China, the total number of IPTV users is 155 million. In 2018, the cumulative traffic of the mobile Internet in China is 71 billion GB, increased by 189.1% when compared with last year (http://www.miit.gov.cn/n1146312/index.html). It is predicted by Cisco that at the end of 2021, 78% of the world's mobile traffic will be mobile multimedia service traffic [1].

Though traffic growth is accompanied by a significant increase in network speed, user satisfaction for multimedia service has not increased significantly. How to perceive and monitor user experience is important. If network operator and content

© The Author(s), under exclusive license to Springer Nature Switzerland AG 2019
X. Wei, L. Zhou, *Multimedia QoE Evaluation*, SpringerBriefs in Computer Science,
https://doi.org/10.1007/978-3-030-23350-1_1

provider can accurately evaluate the user experience during they enjoy service and perform well-directed measurements to promote user feeling, they can achieve huge economic benefits.

The most sensitive, resource-intensive, and promising component in the existing multimedia service is video service. For the video service, there are many factors that affect the user viewing experience, such as video clarity, video content, price, device used by user and the environment, and even the mood of user. The proportions of these factors are different for individual user. In other words, for the same objective environment, the quality of experience of different users is also distinct. Therefore, how to accurately measure users' real experience during video viewing is a difficult but very important issue for operators and content providers. In the research of user experience for video service, it is necessary to explore the important influencing factors from multiple levels and multiple dimensions, so as to obtain an objective and real user experience.

In short, user experience is a key indicator of concern to operators and content providers. Therefore, how to accurately evaluate the response of users to different businesses in different environments has important significance. The current research on user experience is mainly in the laboratory exploration stage. Even if there are a few commercial applications, it does not fully reflect the abstract and subjective user experience. Therefore, research on how to accurately and objectively evaluate the user experience is still a direction worth exploring.

## 1.2  Motivation

Early quality evaluation method mainly studied the abnormality of videos during transmission by the quality of service (QoS) of the network. If the video is abnormal, user experience is poor. On the contrary, if the video has no abnormalities, user experience is better. However, this kind of method can only detect the user experience degradation caused by the network status. They cannot truly reflect the user real feeling. Therefore, in order to quantitatively measure the user experience, the concept of quality of experience (QoE) is proposed for multimedia services.

For the multimedia QoE evaluation, several schemes are proposed, such as subjective evaluation and objective evaluation [2, 3]. The subjective evaluation method obtains user feeling for service through offline questionnaires, telephone surveys, online assessments, and so on. The main research in subjective evaluation is to explore the relationship between QoS and QoE [4]. In [5], the authors proposed a model to measure the impact of coding distortion and packet loss on user experience. In [6], the author mainly discussed the relationship between burst loss rate and user experience, and improved the parametric model based on ITU-T G.1070 video standard. The shortcomings of these subjective evaluations are obvious. Firstly, they require a lot of manpower and material resources to support the experimental operations. Secondly, the subjective evaluation methods can only be tested in the laboratory environment, but not in the real scenarios. There are also many researchers who want to expand the amount of data through crowdsourcing, but the quality of their experiments is often not guaranteed [7].

On the other hand, for the objective evaluation method, it mainly concerns human visual system or reference-based classification methods: full reference type [8], partial reference type [9], and no reference type [10, 11]. In [8], the proposed structural similarity index was a kind of reference-based classification method, which was mainly used to describe the structural difference between original videos and distorted videos after transmission. In addition, a large number of works consider the relationship between QoS and QoE from a psychological perspective [12]. The limitations of the objective evaluation methods are also very obvious. Firstly, when any changes occur in application scenarios, parameters must be re-estimated. Secondly, the objective evaluation model fits the parameters generally through the mean opinion score (MOS) obtained from the subjective test.

In addition, content providers and network operators are not only concerned with the evaluation of user experience, but also its influencing factors. In [13], the author divided the influencing factors into three categories: human-related factors, system-related factors, and context-related factors. Importantly, human-related factor mainly refers to elements caused by the user's own controllable and uncontrollable characteristics. System-related factors refer to technical changes in applications or services that result from the controllable and uncontrollable nature of the technology itself. Context-related factors contain user's location, noise when they enjoy service. It can be perceived through sensors in terminals. However, the factors that are currently proposed by these classification methods are difficult to provide a comprehensive evaluation of multimedia user experience. In other words, impact of the single factor can reflect user experience to some extent the superiority of the factor, but that may be not enough.

## 1.3  Necessity

Through the above introduction, we can know that evaluation for user experience is very important. Existing subjective evaluation method and objective evaluation method still have various defects, which may not be suitable for real application scenarios.

In addition to the above two types of user experience evaluation methods, data-driven methods have been proposed in recent years for further research on video user experience evaluation models [13, 14]. In this kind of methods, multimedia QoE can be evaluated mainly from collected data. However, there are three main issues to be handled when concerning data-driven multimedia QoE evaluation methods:

1. In the era of big data, content providers and network operators can collect massive data from terminals and networks every day. How to preprocess these data and extract key features associated with multimedia QoE are very important. The subjective feature or user-related influencing factors are especially

important. However, due to privacy protection in real application scenarios, information about users cannot be opened. Therefore, several abstract, implicit, and personalized indicators should be mined from the collected data.

2. Unlike traditional modeling and prediction algorithms for processing data from laboratories, data-driven user experience models and prediction algorithms need to handle massive real application dataset [14]. Therefore, it needs to design more appropriate and applicable models and more accurate prediction algorithms, which can integrate subjective and objective influencing factors. Moreover, the property of real time is also a key consideration when deriving QoE modeling and prediction algorithms.

3. When realizing theoretical research results in the big data processing platform, there exists several problems to be solved, such as data collection, storage, analysis, and result demonstration. How to further shorten the gap between theory and practice needs to be paid more attention.

Therefore, it is necessary to study the multimedia QoE evaluation, which builds a QoE model describing relationship between QoE and the related influencing factors through a large amount of real environment data, finally realizing multimedia user QoE prediction. Moreover, how to implement multimedia QoE evaluation in big data processing platform is also crucial. The research of this direction will be of great significance to the development of personalized and interactive multimedia service.

# References

1. Cisco Visual Networking Index (2017) Global mobile data traffic forecast update. 2016–2021 White Paper
2. Chen Y, Wu K, Zhang Q (2015) From QoS to QoE: a tutorial on video quality assessment. IEEE Commun Surv Tut 17(2):1126–1165
3. Skorin-Kapov L, Varela M, Hossfeld T, Chen KT (2018) A survey of emerging concepts and challenges for QoE management of multimedia services. ACM Trans Multimed Comput Commun Appl 14(2s):1–29
4. De Moor K, Ketyko I, Joseph W, Deryckere T, De Marez L, Martens L, Verleye G (2010) Proposed framework for evaluating quality of experience in a mobile, testbed-oriented living lab setting. Mobile Netw Appl 15(3):378–391
5. Zeng AH, Liu J, Xian J (2010) IPTV system architecture and main technologies. Commun Technol 43(3):171–174
6. Reibman AR, Kanumuri S, Vaishampayan V, Cosman PC (2004) Visibility of individual packet losses in MPEG-2 video. In: International conference on image processing, Singapore, Oct 24–27, pp 14–17
7. Cagnini HE, Barros RC, Basgalupp MP (2017) Estimation of distribution algorithms for decision-tree induction. In: IEEE congress on evolutionary computation, Donostia-San Sebastian, June 5–8, pp 2022–2029
8. Seshadrinathan K, Bovik AC (2010) Motion tuned spatio-temporal quality assessment of natural videos. IEEE Trans Image Process 19(2):335–350
9. Rehman A, Wang Z (2012) Reduced-reference image quality assessment by structural similarity estimation. IEEE Trans Image Process 21(8):3378–3389

10. Yang F, Wan S, Xie Q, Wu HR (2010) No-reference quality assessment for networked video via primary analysis of bit stream. IEEE Trans Circuits Syst Video Technol 20(11):1544–1554

11. Lin X, Ma H, Luo L, Chen Y (2012) No-reference video quality assessment in the compressed domain. IEEE Trans Consum Electron 58(2):505–512

12. Usman M, Yang N, Jan MA, He X, Xu M, Lam KM (2018) A joint framework for QoS and QoE for video transmission over wireless multimedia sensor networks. IEEE Trans Mob Comput 17(4):746–759

13. Huang R, Wei X, Zhou L, Lv C, Meng H, Jin J (2018) A survey of data-driven approach on multimedia QoE evaluation. Front Comp Sci 12(6):1060–1075

14. Tu W (2018) Data-driven QoS and QoE management in smart cities: a tutorial study. IEEE Commun Mag 56(12):126–133

# Chapter 2
# Technical Premise

**Abstract** In this chapter, we briefly describe technical premise on multimedia QoE evaluation. Firstly, we present some mainstream definitions about QoE and introduce how to quantify multimedia QoE. Then, we investigate and classify the influencing factors of multimedia QoE from three aspects. Moreover, we introduce existing mainstream multimedia QoE modeling and prediction algorithms based on machine learning. Finally, we give challenges of multimedia QoE evaluation research.

## 2.1 Definition and Quantification

### 2.1.1 Definition of Multimedia QoE

As far as we know, existing literature gives a lot of discussion about QoE definitions, but does not form a unified consensus.

From Wikipedia, it is known that quality of experience (QoE) is "the degree of delight or annoyance of the user of an application or service. It results from the fulfillment of his or her expectations with respect to the utility and/or enjoyment of the application or service in the light of the user's personality and current state" [1]. That is to say, QoE provides an assessment of user experience with respect to a particular service.

ITU-T defines QoE as: "overall acceptability of an application or service, as perceived subjectively by the end user" [2]. Later, European Telecommunications Standards Institute (ETSI) states that "QoE is a measure of user performance based on both objective and subjective psychological measures of using an information communications technology (ICT) service or product" [3].

Moreover, a more comprehensive definition of QoE is proposed by EU Qualinet Community: "QoE is the degree of delight or annoyance of the user of an application or service. It results from the fulfillment of his or her expectations with respect to the utility and/or enjoyment of the application or service in the light of the user's personality and current state" [4].

X. Wei, L. Zhou, *Multimedia QoE Evaluation*, SpringerBriefs in Computer Science, https://doi.org/10.1007/978-3-030-23350-1_2

Based on the above definitions of QoE, multimedia QoE is defined as the user QoE in the domain and applications of multimedia communications and multimedia information processing systems. In other words, multimedia QoE is a subjective feeling, which is generated by the user in the process of interacting with the multimedia service or application.

### 2.1.2  Quantification of Multimedia QoE

In order to concretely describe and evaluate user experience when they enjoy multimedia service, it is important to find the methods of multimedia QoE quantification. Category scale, sequential scale, and isometric scale are usually adopted to measure multimedia QoE. Here, we introduce three main multimedia QoE quantification measurements.

1. Acceptable/Unacceptable

Multimedia QoE can be divided into two categories: acceptable and unacceptable [5, 6].

2. Mean opinion score (MOS)

One of the most well-known methods for evaluating multimedia QoE is called the mean opinion score (MOS) rating test, which is proposed by ITU [7]. It divides the user subjective feeling in the multimedia service into five levels, from bad to excellent. As shown in Table 2.1, this quantitative method describes the user subjective feeling in detail, belonging to a sequential scale method.

3. Paired comparison score

In [8], the paired comparison method is used to quantify QoE, which belongs to the isometric scale method. The general idea of the paired comparison method is as follows: firstly, it needs to prepare $N$ samples. Subsequently, let users select and compare two samples among $N$ each time. That is to say, users should jointly perform $M = C_N^2$ comparisons, and record the results of each comparison. Finally, it performs the Bradley–Terry–Luce model to process the results of $M$ comparisons, and then gives a score for each sample.

**Table 2.1** Mean opinion score [7]

| MOS | QoE | Degree of damage |
|---|---|---|
| 5 | Excellent | Undetectable |
| 4 | Good | Can detect, but not serious |
| 3 | Fair | Slight |
| 2 | Poor | Serious |
| 1 | Bad | Very serious |

**Table 2.2**  The comparison of three measurements  [9]

| Quantization measurement | Advantages | Disadvantages |
|---|---|---|
| Acceptable/Unacceptable | Simple, user-friendly, high accuracy | The description of the users' subjective feelings is not detailed enough |
| MOS | A more detailed description of the user subjective feeling | The boundaries between several levels are vague, and different people have different understandings towards these levels |
| Paired comparison score | The number of quality levels can vary. The evaluation results given by the user can be consistently verified and the accuracy is high | Heavy workload |

The above three quantization measurements have their own advantages and disadvantages, summarized in Table 2.2. Obviously, the acceptable/unacceptable label is simple and accurate, but its granularity is rough in several cases. The paired comparison score is more accurate than the MOS, but it requires a lot of work to obtain scores. For example, if there are 20 test samples, MOS is obtained by performing only 20 judgments, while the paired comparison score is achieved by performing 190 judgments.

Considering the above-mentioned advantages and disadvantages of different measurements, MOS is still the most widely used quantification measurement for representing and evaluating multimedia QoE.

## 2.2  Influencing Factors

As multimedia QoE is the level of user subjective feeling in multimedia service, it is prone to be influenced by several factors. Therefore, the study of the influencing factors (IFs) is critical when evaluating multimedia QoE. As mentioned in  [5], influencing factor is defined as characteristics of a user, system, service, application, or context whose actual state or setting may have influence on that user's QoE. That is to say, all aspects of these factors may influence user QoE. Moreover, some of these factors are related, not isolated completely. In general, these IFs can be summarized into three main categories: (1) system-related IFs; (2) context-related IFs; (3) user-related IFs  [10, 11]. The first two categories belong to objective QoE factors, while the last category belongs to subjective QoE factors.

Typical IFs of multimedia QoE are enumerated in Table 2.3 and will be discussed in detail below.

**Table 2.3** Representative influencing factors of multimedia QoE [11]

| Category | Typical QoE Influencing factors |
|---|---|
| System-related IFs | Content-related: spatial–temporal requirements, color depth, 2D/3D, texture, content reliability, etc. |
| | Media-related: encoding, resolution, sampling rate, frame rate, etc. |
| | Network-related: bandwidth, delay, jitter, packet loss rate, error rate, throughput, etc. |
| | Device-related: memory, battery life, screen size, CPU usage, etc. |
| Context-related IFs | Physical: location, space, movements, etc. |
| | Temporal: collection time, duration, frequency of use, etc. |
| | Economic: costs, subscription type, brand, etc. |
| | Task/social: multitasking situation/social occasion, etc. |
| | Service type: live video, video on demand, time-shift video, etc. |
| User-related IFs | Low-level processing: gender, age, education degree, character, etc. |
| | High-level processing: interest, viewing habit, viewing behavior, emotion, tolerance for video playing delay, caching and advertisements, etc. |

## 2.2.1  System-Related Influencing Factors

System-related IFs refer to properties and characteristics that determine the technically produced quality of an application or service. In multimedia service, system-related IFs can be further divided into four types: content-related IFs, media-related IFs, network-related IFs, and device-related IFs.

More detail, content-related IFs mainly include content type and content reliability, such as specific temporal or spatial requirements, color depth, texture, 2D/3D. In [12], the impacts of spatial–temporal resolutions and quantization step size were modeled by inverted falling exponential functions. The color depth was studied for high dynamic range (HDR) videos in [13]. In [14], a quality model for depth information of 3D stereoscopic videos was developed.

Media-related IFs, such as encoding, resolution, sampling rate, frame rate, media synchronization, contribute to media-related IFs. In [15], the authors studied and quantified the influences of video resolution, scaling method, video frame rate, and video content types on the QoE. In [16], Buchinger et al. described the interconnection between compression rate and frame rate in mobile environments. It turned out that, for a given resolution, users preferred a video with higher image quality, i.e., lower compression rate, and low frame rate instead of a video with medium picture quality and high frame rate. In the experiments, they tested videos on desktop computers and palmtops in two different resolutions, $352 \times 244$ for the desktop experiments and $176 \times 144$ for the palmtop experiments. They confirmed that users tended to neglect a reduction of the frame rate in palmtops. Similar investigations were carried out in [17].

Network-related IFs mainly refer to data transmission over a network [4]. As far as we known, QoS is the most popular system quality strategy used to measure the performance of a service, such as bandwidth, delay (depends on network capacity), jitter (refers to irregular delays), packet loss (due to unreliable transmission), error rate, throughput. Some references focus on the impact of these IFs on QoS, while the others try to establish the relationship of these network-related IFs and QoE [18–22].

Device-related IFs refer to the devices involved in the service that includes system specifications (e.g., personalization), equipment specifications (e.g., mobility), device capabilities (e.g., display screen, battery), and provider specification and capabilities. It is known that subjective results provided by mobile users with different devices can be highly different even though they are viewing the same video sequence in the same environment. In [23], the authors studied the impacts of video resolution, viewing device, and audio quality on the perceived audiovisual quality. In [24], the authors analyzed the impact of interactivity and introduced it into the objective QoE model. In [25], the authors studied the impacts of smartphone configurations, including CPU, screen size, and display resolution, on the QoE of end users in the context of multi-party video conference.

## 2.2.2 Context-Related Influencing Factors

Context-related IFs are factors that embrace any situational property to describe user's environment in terms of physical, temporal, social, economic, task, and service type characteristics.

Physical context illustrates location and space characteristics, including movements within and transitions between locations. In [26], quality of full-length movies and video fragments was evaluated by integrating physical context factor.

Temporal context is also an important component, focusing on the time-related factors covering the time of day for playing, duration, and frequency of playing. The study of [27] investigated whether the quality perception and rating behavior changed with the adjustment of video durations. They observed that long clips (60, 120, and 240 s) were rated slightly higher than the short ones (10, 15, and 30 s), especially for the videos of high visual qualities. The test in [28] concluded that most mobile videos were watched in the afternoon and evening at home.

Economic context can also influence multimedia QoE, which involves costs, subscription type, or brand of the service/system. The influences of quality, payment, and content choices on QoE were investigated in [29]. The authors found a positive feedback of QoE when the users were free to choose video contents based on their own preferences. However, this positive feedback was not observed when the users were asked to pay more money for high quality videos. The situation went worse when users were given low quality videos but asked to pay the same amount of money as high quality ones. They also discovered that an increase to the price of the same content may lower the user experience of video quality.

As well known that one of the most important features is human sociality. The social context, such as alone or with other person during viewing, describes scenario involved in the research.

Moreover, multimedia service type, such as live service, video on demand (VoD), and time-shift service, has also influence on user QoE. Specifically live videos in the TV or network are broadcasted for all of users in fixed time. VoD is the videos selected by users according to their interests. Time-shift videos are recent live videos which can be replaying by users.

### 2.2.3   User-Related Influencing Factors

User-related IFs are any variant or invariant properties or characteristics of a user. The characteristics can describe the demographic and socio-economic background, the physical and mental constitution, or user's emotional state. Existing research about user-related IFs are listed and compared in Table 2.4.

From the above table we can see, as user-related IFs are subjective and abstract, they are hard to be collected and extracted. Existing methods such as collection by special monitoring devices or questionnaires are only suitable in laboratory environment. Moreover, due to privacy protection in real application scenarios, user's age, gender, character cannot be obtained. Therefore, how to extract user-related IFs from big data in real applications is an important issue to be handled.

In summary, we have analyzed multimedia QoE IFs from system-related, context-related, and user-related aspects. However, compared with system-related IFs, the works for context-related IFs and user-related IFs are still limited. Moreover, how to describe the subjective IFs, especially user-related IFs, from objective manners is important but difficult. We have performed several exploratory works in this field, which will be described in Chap. 3.

**Table 2.4**  User-related IFs and their extraction methods

| Reference | User-related IFs—extraction method | Application |
|---|---|---|
| [30] | (1) Age—given; (2) enjoyment, engagement—questionnaire | Video conference |
| [31] | (1) User's interaction behavior—collected by developed GUI; (2) age, gender—given | VoD in lab |
| [32, 33] | User's viewing behavior (eye movements and blinks)—by video camera; | VoD in lab |
| [34] | (1) Social context—questionnaire; (2) enjoyment, engagement—questionnaire | VoD in lab |
| [35] | (1) Video content—collected by terminal devices; (2) user's viewing behavior—collected by terminal devices | VoD in Internet |
| [36] | User's blood pressure, heartbeat—collected by Somatosensory monitoring devices | VoIP in lab |
| [37] | User's waiting time and service time—analysis | OTT |

## 2.3  Multimedia QoE Evaluation Based on Machine Learning

Multimedia QoE evaluation is to obtain or measure user experience/feeling according to subjective, objective, or data-driven methods. On one hand, subjective test directly measures QoE by asking users to give their scores for the equality of multimedia services under test. It is time consuming and expensive. The test can only be performed in a laboratory not in real environments. On the other hand, in objective methods, some algorithms are used to test video quality or find the relationship between QoS and QoE. These algorithms do not consider the context-related and user-related IFs. Additionally, they are not fit for the big multimedia data and application scenario. Data-driven multimedia QoE evaluation algorithm realizes QoE modeling and prediction by analyzing the collected dataset. Moreover, existing representative multimedia QoE evaluation algorithms can be divided into algorithms based on statistics, algorithms based on psychology, algorithms based on machine learning. In this subsection, we briefly introduce algorithms based on machine learning, containing model establishment and training and prediction algorithms design [38].

### 2.3.1  Decision Tree

Decision tree (DT) is a model of hierarchical tree structure. Each intermediate node selects a property (that is, an IF in the QoE evaluation problem) and deploys a test based on that property, while each leaf node represents a decision (type/tag). DT is widely used in predicting QoE [39–42]. In [39], a QoE model was built by decision tree and prediction was realized. One weakness of DT was that they are not fitted for processing the continuous IFs. Therefore, fuzzy decision tree combining DT with fuzzy theory was introduced in [40]. It was able to handle continuous IFs. Specifically, in [40], data was collected from top five popular video sites in China and the key quality metrics of session such as join time, frame rate, bandwidth, buffering times, buffering ratio were extracted. Among them, playing ratio was selected for measuring user QoE. Finally, fuzzy decision tree was built in four steps: (1) preprocess the data; (2) induce a fuzzy decision tree; (3) turn the fuzzy decision tree into a collection of fuzzy rules; (4) classify records with unknown class based on the fuzzy rules.

DT can also be used to evaluate online multimedia QoE [41]. In [41], Hoeffding option trees (HOT) and Oza Bagging HOT were used to build online multimedia QoE prediction model. By adding nodes combining multiple models, HOT can effectively reduce evaluation error rate. Oza Bagging HOT, an online learning ensemble method, was used to get better performance and improve the generalization ability compared with the standalone classifiers.

In [42], an end-to-end QoE prediction model for video streaming service in LTE networks was proposed. The proposed QoE model was based in gradient boosting

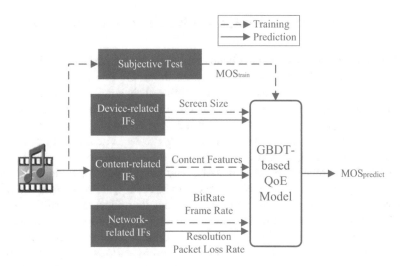

**Fig. 2.1** The GBDT-based QoE evaluation model [42]

decision tree (GBDT) with IFs from cross layer, network layer (package loss rate), application layer (bit rate, frame rate), and user equipment (screen size, video resolution), shown in Fig. 2.1. It contained training process and predicting process. In the training process, objective cross-layer parameters in combination with subjective MOS values were used to train $M$ base learners with good generalization ability. In the predicting process, only objective parameters were available, and the predicted QoE values were obtained from the well-trained model.

## 2.3.2  Support Vector Machine

Support vector machine (SVM) is a supervised learning model widely used for classification and regression. It uses a series of hyperplanes which maximize the distance between the nearest training data points among the classes. In [43], a QoE model based on SVM was proposed to measure HTTP video streaming service in wireless networks. SVM can be also combined with other methods such as video quality metrics (VQM) [44]. The proposed model had higher correlation with MOS than G.1070 and G.1070E.

Since support vector machines (SVM) are a two-class classification problem, there is a limitation to using SVM for QoE evaluation that it can only divide QoE into two aspects, acceptable and unacceptable.

### 2.3.3   Artificial Neural Network

ANN is constructed by large nonlinear, adaptive processing unites. Many researchers have applied ANN on building QoE model, obtaining high accuracy [45, 46]. In [45], a QoE model based on neural networks (NNs) was proposed. The authors integrated the back propagation neural network (BPNN) with particle swarm optimization (PSO) to predict user QoE. Specifically, the BPNN can improve computational complexity and learn by itself. PSO was used to adjust result from BPNN to optimize the accuracy. There were two main steps in the proposed methods: Firstly, it chose a neural network and trained the weights of that model. Then, the model was used to predict QoE, taking mean squared error (MSE) as evaluation indicators. During this process, PSO was used to fine tune the weights of neural network for further reducing MSE.

In [46], radial basis function networks (RBFNs) were used to build QoE model over wireless networks. One advantage of the RBFN based QoE model was that it can obtain higher Pearson correlation than the other three methods (KNN, G.1070, BPNN) with low computational complexity.

### 2.3.4   Bayesian Network

Bayesian network is a directed acyclic graph where each node is represented with quantitative probability information. Bayesian network has good capability to handle problems with high uncertainty. In this scheme, Bayesian network is usually used for building the relationship between objective QoE IFs and subjective QoE IFs to be inferred. Finally, the inferred subjective QoE IFs are converted into MOS according to several mapping rules. An example of representative Bayesian network was proposed in [47]. In this example, the relationship between abstract subjective QoE IFs (user satisfaction and technology acceptance) and objective QoE IFs (bandwidth, location, packet loss, delay) can be built by directed edges in the Bayesian network.

In [48], a context aware model for measuring QoE over time was proposed. The model used the state space approach and combined dynamic Bayesian networks to measure user QoE. Expectation maximization algorithm was used to learn parameters of the dynamic Bayesian networks. In [18], the authors used Bayesian network to build a unified model to represent and explain QoE of mobile VoD. In [49], Bayesian network is suggested for building QoE model on P2P live streaming systems by user-related IFs and context-related IFs. However, the limitation of Bayesian network is that it needs to explicitly set the relationships when designing model structure.

### 2.3.5   Hidden Markov Model

Hidden Markov model (HMM) is widely used in many applications, ranging from speech recognition to human activity recognition system. The main characteristic of HMM is that it takes model of measuring multimedia QoE as a time series model. As the current QoE or IFs are effected by previous QoE or IFs, HMM can be used to model the time series characteristic of multimedia QoE [50, 51].

In [50], an emotion-assisted QoE assessment model was built with HMM and DT. User emotion was defined as six moods: happy, relaxed, afraid, angry, sad, bored, and real-time emotional model was built with HMM. The emotional attributes of the video content were identified and matching degree was used to represent the difference between emotions of user and video content emotion. It was noted that the matching degree was defined as three levels: high, medium, and low. Finally, matching degree, average bitrate, and buffer ratio were taken as input to build QoE model with DT. In [51], user experience of adaptive video streaming was improved with a prediction mechanism based on HMM. The prediction results for throughput can effectively improve the user QoE of adaptive video streaming.

### 2.3.6   Other Models

From models mentioned above, DT is very popular in modeling for evaluation of multimedia QoE. Moreover, there are still other methods and discussion about building models in multimedia QoE evaluation. In [52, 53], Bayesian statistical method was firstly used for measuring QoE on interactive audiovisual communications. In [54], the authors proposed the MLQoE model. It employed the SVM, ANN, DT, and Gaussian Naive Bayes classifiers and found the best prediction model automatically.

There is great space for developing dynamic model for multimedia QoE evaluation. In other words, most of multimedia QoE evaluation approaches do not take the time characteristic of QoE into consideration. For example, if a user gets a low QoE in one moment, he may continue to watch the video if he gets a high QoE in next moment. If a user gets several consecutive low QoE moments, he is more likely to quit in the middle of view. Therefore, QoE may vary over time. Moreover, some key IFs are also changing during the view process such as user mood, status of device, and so on. It should pay more attention to time characteristics of IFs and QoE specially in real-time QoE monitoring scenarios.

Moreover, many advanced analysis tools can be leveraged to give a more accurate QoE prediction. For example, most of the previous QoE models just consider about base learners. Ensemble methods always get much better generalization ability than base learners. Building QoE model based on ensemble methods deserves further investigations. Deep learning algorithms [55, 56] can help extract important QoS and external factors that contribute to user QoE. It can be also adopted to describe complex QoS-QoE relationships.

## 2.4   Challenges

1. Multimedia QoE evaluation challenges related to data collection and feature extraction

Data collection and feature extraction are basic, but very important tasks of multimedia QoE evaluation. In data collection, there is no unified statement or consensus on the collected types of data. For example, equipment or eye tracker that monitors user's expression is expensive. Subjective questionnaire/user score may not be accurate for user QoE. How to collect data in a cheap but effective way is worth discussing. Moreover, as the amount of data is usually huge and there exists missing data, how to effectively store and clean them is also troublesome.

Another challenge is feature extraction. How to extract valuable features closely related to user experience from the collected and preprocessed data is vital for the following modeling and evaluation procedure. It is noted that some context-related IFs and user-related IFs are abstract and subjective, how to obtain and mine them from data has become a hot topic in this field.

2. Multimedia QoE evaluation challenges related to modeling and prediction

Building appropriate models and designing associated prediction algorithm are key steps to perform multimedia QoE evaluation. Firstly, as the relationships among IFs or features are complex and sometimes implicit, the designed models need to have ability to describe these relations. Moreover, the selected or designed models can be able to accurately set up the connection between IFs and multimedia QoE. Secondly, as the big data exist and data itself may be heterogeneous, the designed model needs to handle these issues.

For the design model training and prediction algorithms, the challenges are embodied in how to derive the simple and efficient algorithms. Furthermore, for the real-time requirement, how to design online training and prediction algorithms also becomes key challenges. The computation complexity of algorithms in real application scenarios needs to be further reduced.

3. Multimedia QoE challenges related to the implementation

Although several theoretical research results in multimedia QoE evaluation have emerged, the implementation of those results on big data processing platform is still blank. Specifically, how to design a comprehensive, efficient, reliable, and accurate open big data analysis and processing prototype system is a challenge. Furthermore, how to demonstrate the evaluation results in real applications is also an important problem to be solved.

## 2.5  Summary

In this chapter, we describe technical premise and overview the state-of-the-art research works of multimedia QoE evaluation. Firstly, we conclude the mainstream multimedia QoE definitions and introduce the quantitative methods of multimedia QoE. Then, we discuss multimedia QoE influencing factors from three aspects in a systematic way. Subsequently, we introduce existing multimedia QoE modeling and prediction algorithms based on machine learning. Finally, we point out challenges of multimedia QoE evaluation research and implementation.

## References

1. Quality of experience. http://www.wikepedia.org
2. ITU Telecommunication Standardization Sector and OF ITU (2007) Definition of quality of experience (QoE). ITU-T Recommendation P.10/G.100
3. European Telecommunication Standards Institute TC HF (Human Factors) (2010) Quality of Experience (QoE) requirements for real-time communication services. Technical report, European Telecommunication Standards Institute
4. Callet PL, Moller S, Perkis A (2013) Qualinet white paper on definitions of quality of experience (QoE)
5. Chen Y, Wu K, Zhang Q (2015) From QoS to QoE: a tutorial on video quality assessment. IEEE Commun Surv Tut 17(2):1126–1165
6. Menkovski V, Oredope A, Liotta A, Sánchez AC (2009) Predicting quality of experience in multimedia streaming. In: Proceedings of the 7th International Conference on Advances in Mobile Computing and Multimedia, Kuala Lumpur, Dec 14–16, pp 52–59
7. ITU-T Rec (2006) P. 800.1, mean opinion score (MOS) terminology. International Telecommunication Union
8. Chen KT, Wu CC, Chang YC, Lei CL (2009) A crowd source-able QoE evaluation framework for multimedia content. In: Proceedings of the 17th ACM international conference on multimedia, Beijing, Oct 19–24, pp 491–500
9. Lin C, Hu J, Kong X (2012) Survey on models and evaluation of quality of experience. Chin J Comput 35(1):1–15
10. Skorin-Kapov L, Varela M, Hossfeld T, Chen KT (2018) A survey of emerging concepts and challenges for QoE management of multimedia services. ACM Trans Multimed Comput Commun Appl 14(2s):1–29
11. Zhao T, Liu Q, Chen CW (2017) QoE in video transmission: a user experience-driven strategy. IEEE Commun Surv Tut 19(1):285–302
12. Ou YF, Xue Y, Wang Y (2014) Q-star: a perceptual video quality model considering impact of spatial, temporal, and amplitude resolutions. IEEE Trans Image Process 23(6):2473–2486
13. Thoma H, de-Frutos-López M, Auer J (2013) Chroma subsampling for HDR video with improved subjective quality. In: Picture Coding Symposium, San Jose, CA, Dec 8–11, pp 345–348
14. Lebreton P, Raake A, Barkowsky M, Le Callet P (2012) Evaluating depth perception of 3D stereoscopic videos. IEEE J Sel Top Sign Proces 6(6):710–720
15. Zinner T, Hohlfeld O, Abboud O, Hossfeld T (2010) Impact of frame rate and resolution on objective QoE metrics. In: International workshop on quality of multimedia experience, Trondheim, June 21–23, pp 1–8
16. Buchinger S, Hlavacs H (2006) Subjective quality of mobile MPEG-4 videos with different frame rates. J Mob Multimed 1(4):327–341

17. Zeina S, Conrad BA (2019) Large-scale study of perceptual video quality. IEEE Trans Image Process 28(2):612–627
18. Wang Y, Li P, Jiao L, Su Z, Cheng N, Shen XS, Zhang P (2017) A data-driven architecture for personalized QoE management in 5G wireless networks. IEEE Wirel Commun 24(1):102–110
19. Sackl A, Casas P, Schatz R, Janowski L, Irmer R (2015) Quantifying the impact of network bandwidth fluctuations and outages on Web QoE. In: International Workshop on Quality of Multimedia Experience, Pylos, May 26–29, pp 1–6
20. Zhou L (2017) QoE-driven delay announcement for cloud mobile media. IEEE Trans Circuits Syst Video Technol 27(1):84–94
21. Aguilera N, Bustos J, Lalanne F (2016) Adkintun mobile: study of relation between QoS and QoE in mobile networks. IEEE Lat Am Trans 14(6):2770–2772
22. Xu S, Wang X, Huang M (2018) Modular and deep QoE/QoS mapping for multimedia services over satellite networks. Int J Commun Syst 31(17):e3793
23. Sidaty NO, Larabi MC, Saadane A (2014) Influence of video resolution, viewing device and audio quality on perceived multimedia quality for steaming applications. In: 5th European workshop on visual information processing, Paris, Dec 10–12, pp 1–6
24. Floris A, Atzori L, Ginesu G (2015) The impact of interactivity on the QoE: a preliminary analysis. In: IEEE international conference on communication workshop, London, June 8–12, pp 1711–1716
25. Vucic D, Skorin-Kapov L (2015) The impact of mobile device factors on QoE for multi-party video conferencing via WebRTC. In: 13th international conference on telecommunications (Contel), Inffeldgasse 12, Graz, July 13–15, pp 1–8
26. Van den Broeck W, Jacobs A, Staelens N (2012) Integrating the everyday-life context in subjective video quality experiments. In: Fourth international workshop on quality of multimedia experience, Melbourne, VIC, July 5–7, pp 19–24
27. Frohlich P, Egger S, Schatz R, Muhlegger M, Masuch K, Gardlo B (2012) QoE in 10 seconds: are short video clip lengths sufficient for quality of experience assessment? In: Fourth international workshop on quality of multimedia experience, Melbourne, VIC, July 5–7, pp 242–247
28. De Pessemier T, Martens L, Joseph W (2013) Modeling subjective quality evaluations for mobile video watching in a living lab context. In: IEEE international symposium on broadband multimedia systems and broadcasting, London, June 4–7, pp 1–5
29. Sackl A, Zwickl P, Reichl P (2013) The trouble with choice: an empirical study to investigate the influence of charging strategies and content selection on QoE. In: Proceedings of the 9th international conference on network and service management, Zurich, Oct 14–18, pp 298–303
30. Schmitt M, Redi J, Bulterman D, Cesar PS (2018) Towards individual QoE for multiparty videoconferencing. IEEE Trans Multimedia 20(7):1781–1795
31. Tasaka S (2017) Bayesian hierarchical regression models for QoE estimation and prediction in audiovisual communications. IEEE Trans Multimedia 19(6):1195–1208
32. Song J, Yang F, Zhou Y, Wan S, Wu HR (2016) QoE evaluation of multimedia services based on audiovisual quality and user interest. IEEE Trans Multimedia 18(3):444–457
33. Arndt S, Radun J, Antons JN, Sebastian M (2014) Using eye-tracking and correlates of brain activity to predict quality scores. In: 6th international workshop on quality of multimedia experience, Singapore, Sep 18–20, pp 281–285
34. Zhu Y, Heynderickx I, Redi JA (2015) Understanding the role of social context and user factors in video quality of experience. Comput Hum Behav 49:412–426
35. Yue T, Wang H, Cheng S (2018) Learning from users: a data-driven method of QoE evaluation for internet video. Multimed Tools Appl 77(20):27269–27300
36. Mitra K, Zaslavsky A, Ahlund C (2015) Context-aware QoE modelling, measurement, and prediction in mobile computing systems. IEEE Trans Mob Comput 14(5):920–936
37. Xu Y, Xiao Z, Feng H, Yang T, Hu B, Zhou Y (2017) Modeling buffer starvations of video streaming in cellular networks with large-scale measurement of user behavior. IEEE Trans Mob Comput 16(8):2228–2245

38. Huang R, Wei X, Zhou L, Lv C, Meng H, Jin J (2018) A survey of data-driven approach on multimedia QoE evaluation. Front Comp Sci 12(6):1060–1075
39. Balachandran A, Sekar V, Akella A, Seshan S, Stoica I, Hui Z (2013) Developing a predictive model of quality of experience for internet video. In: ACM conference on applications, technologies, architectures, and protocols for computer communication, Hong Kong, Aug 12–16, pp 339–350
40. Zhang Y, Yue T, Wang H, Wei A (2014) Predicting the quality of experience for Internet video with fuzzy decision tree. In: IEEE 17th international conference on computational science and engineering, Chengdu, Dec 19–21, pp 1181–1187
41. Menkovski V, Exarchakos G, Liotta A (2010) Online QoE prediction. In: Second International Workshop on Quality of Multimedia Experience (QoMEX), Trondheim, June 21–23, pp 118–123
42. Chen H, Yu X, Xie L (2013) End-to-end quality adaptation scheme based on QoE prediction for video streaming service in LTE networks. In: 11th international symposium and workshops on modeling and optimization in mobile, ad hoc and wireless networks, Tsukuba Science City, May 13–17, pp 627–633
43. Qian L, Chen H, Xie L (2015) SVM-based QoE estimation model for video streaming service over wireless networks. In: International conference on wireless communications & signal processing. Nanjing, Oct 15–17, pp 1–6
44. Wang B, Zou D, Ding R (2011) Support vector regression based video quality prediction. In: IEEE international symposium on multimedia, Dana point, CA, Dec 5–7, pp 476–481
45. Zheng K, Zhang X, Zheng Q, Xiang W, Hanzo L (2015) Quality-of-experience assessment and its application to video services in LTE networks. IEEE Wirel Commun 22(1):70–78
46. Kang Y, Chen H, Xie L (2013) An artificial-neural-network-based QoE estimation model for Video streaming over wireless networks. In: IEEE/CIC International Conference on Communications in China, Xi'an, Aug 12–14, pp 264–269
47. Mitra K, Zaslavsky A, Åhlund C (2015) Context-aware QoE modelling, measurement, and prediction in mobile computing systems. IEEE Trans Mob Comput 14(5):920–936
48. Mitra K, Zaslavsky A, Åhlund C (2011) Dynamic Bayesian networks for sequential quality of experience modelling and measurement. In: Smart Spaces and Next Generation Wired/Wireless Networking. Springer, Berlin, pp 135–146
49. Mian AU, Hu Z, Tian H (2013) Estimation of in-service quality of experience for peer-to-peer live video streaming systems using a user-centric and context-aware approach based on Bayesian networks. Trans Emerg Telecommun Technol 24(3):280–287
50. Chen M, Hao Y, Mao S, Wu D, Zhou Y (2016) User intent-oriented video QoE with emotion detection networking. In: IEEE Global Communications Conference, Washington, Dec 4–8, pp 1–6
51. Sun Y, Yin X, Wang N, Jiang J, Sekar V, Jin Y, Sinopoli B (2015) Analyzing TCP throughput stability and predictability with implications for adaptive video streaming. Preprint. arXiv:1506.05541
52. Tasaka S (2017) Bayesian hierarchical regression models for QoE estimation and prediction in audiovisual communications. IEEE Trans Multimedia 19(6):1195–1208
53. Tasaka, S (2019) Bayesian categorical modeling of multidimensional QoE in haptic-audiovisual communications. In: IEEE international conference on communications, Shanghai, May 20–22, pp 1–6
54. Charonyktakis P, Plakia M, Tsamardinos I, Papadopouli M (2016) On user-centric modular QoE prediction for VoIP based on machine-learning algorithms. IEEE Trans Mobile Comput 15(6):1443–1456
55. He X, Wang K, Huang H, Liu B (2018) QoE-driven big data architecture for smart city. IEEE Commun Mag 56(2):88–93
56. Bampis CG, Li Z, Katsavounidis I, Bovik AC (2018) Recurrent and dynamic models for predicting streaming video quality of experience. IEEE Trans. Image Process 27(7):3316–3331

# Chapter 3
# Multimedia Service Data Preprocessing and Feature Extraction

**Abstract** In this chapter, we focus on the multimedia service data preprocessing and feature extraction, which are core steps in the multimedia QoE evaluation. Specifically, multimedia service data collection and preprocessing is firstly introduced. We briefly describe three representative datasets: (1) IPTV service dataset collected by operator; (2) OTT service dataset collected from students in Nanjing University of Posts and Telecommunications; (3) dataset crawled across the web. Then, we highlight our works about feature extractions for user-related IFs, containing five aspects: viewing time ratio calculation, user interest inference, user type classification, user behavior analysis, and user emotion parsing from their comments in danmaku.

## 3.1 Multimedia Service Data Collection and Preprocessing

### 3.1.1 IPTV Service Dataset

Recently, with the development of multimedia service and IPTV technology, the proliferation of network users, how to obtain useful information from the huge amount of collected data has become a key issue for IPTV operators. Here, the IPTV service dataset collected from an operator in China consists of two main parts. One is the uploading monitoring data from terminal IPTV set-top boxes, while the other part is fault maintenance data from user's proactive complaint due to various network and service failures. The specific size of this dataset is shown in Fig. 3.1.

Specifically, for the operator, it has more than 600,000 IPTV daily active users, and terminal set-top boxes upload huge number of viewing records to the server every day. Specifically, an average of $1T$ data-level viewing records are collected every month. As shown in Fig. 3.1, there are about 100 million pieces of data detected by the set-top box every day, about 1200 pieces of fault repair data, and about 7000 pieces of programs viewed by users. For each data, it contains several fields, whose meanings are provided in Table 3.1.

For the fault maintenance data, it means the returned user complaint. The reasons and the related percentage over 25,448 complaints are summarized in Table 3.2.

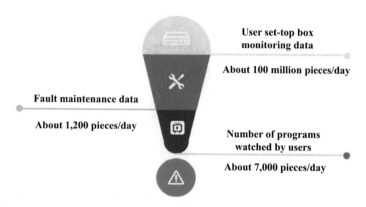

**Fig. 3.1** The size of the IPTV service dataset

From this table we can see, "edge node failure" caused by the network side accounts for 32.99%, "broadband network failure" accounts for 25.43%, and the remaining terminals and users reasons account for 41.58%. Therefore, the edge node fault needs to be checked and solved firstly when the complaints happen.

Furthermore, in the 8359 "edge node failure" complaints, "pause/crash" accounts for 26.84%, "no image" accounts for 25.90%. The remaining part is a variety of error codes, such as "other error codes," "error 10071," "error 1304," etc.

## 3.1.2   OTT Service Dataset

As we all know, the traditional QoE measurement method only considers objective IFs such as QoS, ignoring the subjective IFs on multimedia QoE. In addition, there are certain limitations in measuring user subjective QoE. In view of the shortcomings of traditional QoE, in order to construct a hybrid QoE model with subjective and objective IFs as parameters to predict the actual QoE of users, we collect OTT service data from a part of students from Nanjing University of Posts and Telecommunications. Specifically, the collected data are from two aspects. One is to use the free routers in the dormitory, classroom, and laboratory to collect the data belonging to objective IFs when the selected students enjoy video services. The other is to use questionnaires to gather user's identity, habit, and preference.

1. Data collected from routers

We deploy 50 routers in the campus of Nanjing University of Posts and Telecommunications for data collection. For each router, it can be connected by many terminals at the same time. A person may also have multiple terminals. In order to control data from routers, we have established a complete automatic data collection and storage platform.

**Table 3.1**  The meaning of each field in the data uploaded by the IPTV set-top box

| Field | Meaning |
| --- | --- |
| ALARM_SEVERITY | Alarm level |
| ALARM_NUMBER | Number of alarms |
| PACKET_LOSS_RATE | Packet loss rate |
| STB_DOWN_BANDWIDTH | Downlink bandwidth |
| BITRATE | Bitrate |
| MEDIA_LOSSRATE | Number of media packets lost per second |
| NETWORK_CONDITION | Current network status |
| CPU_USAGE_RATE | CPU usage rate |
| CHANNEL_ONLINE_DURATION | Channel playing duration |
| ONLINE_DURATION | Cumulative playing duration |
| ALARM_DURATION | Cumulative alarm duration |
| PAUSE_NUM | Pause number |
| PAUSE_DURATION | Pause duration |
| BUFFER_SIZE | Buffer size |
| BTV_NUM | Number of lives |
| BTV_FAILURE | Number of live broadcast failures |
| JITTER | Jitter |
| DELAY | Delay |
| AVAILABLE_RATE | Available rate |
| ONLINE_DURATION | Playing duration of program |
| SWITCH_DURATION | Switching time |
| REQUIRE | Number of requests |
| ONLINE_FAILURE | Total number of playback errors |
| SWITCH_NUM | Switching times |
| SWITCH_FAILURE | Number of switching failures |
| SWITCH_DELAY | Switching average delay |
| SWITCH_DELAY_SUCCESS | Number of times the switching delay reaches the standard |
| VOD_NUM | Number of VODs |
| VOD_FAILURE | Number of VOD failures |
| VOD_DELAY | Average VOD delay |
| VOD_DELAY_SUCCESS | Number of times the on-demand delay reaches the standard |
| BTV_DELAY | Average live delay |
| VOD_DELAY_SUCCESS | Number of times the on-demand delay reaches the standard |
| BTV_DELAY_SUCCESS | Number of times the live broadcast delay reaches the standard |

**Table 3.2** The reason and their percentage of complaints

| Reason | Percentage |
| --- | --- |
| Edge node failure | 32.99% |
| Broadband network failure | 25.43% |
| User error | 11.67% |
| User terminal fault/Home gateway failure | 10.95% |
| Reset/restart the set-top box | 9.76% |
| The cable of the set-top box is loose/damaged/not energized | 9.20% |

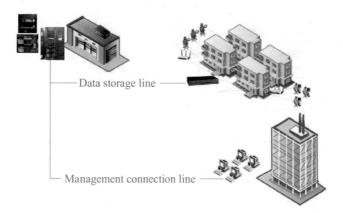

**Fig. 3.2** Data storage and management connections

Generally, we create a specific numbered folder for each router on the IBMV7000 storage array. After the data reaches a certain size, it automatically interrupts the acquisition and restarts the new acquisition. By observing the collection situation, we can know the running status of each router. The data storage and management connection circuits are shown in Fig. 3.2.

Specifically, data collection phase has been divided into two parts: packet capture and router information. These two parts are executed simultaneously. In the data collection phase, packet capture process is firstly started by using the "nohup+&" command, and then router information in the current phase is obtained. Moreover, tcpdump is used to copy all packets forwarded by the router. When the packet is accumulated to a certain amount, it will be saved in the PCAP file format and then sent to the specified directory of NFS.

The collected data is stored on the NFS server via the Nanjing University of Posts and Telecommunications campus network. The whole network structure is shown in Fig. 3.3. The data collected by the router reaches the NFS management server through the campus network gateway and the rack switch.

We extract various video parameters when performing packet interception analysis on different video sites, including Youku APP, Web Youku, Potato Video, Iqiyi Video, Tencent Video. The parameters extracted from these video sites are shown in Table 3.3.

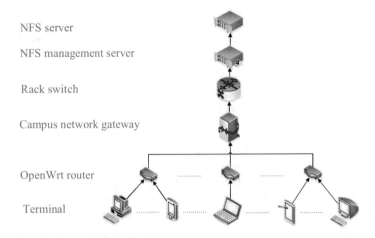

NFS server

NFS management server

Rack switch

Campus network gateway

OpenWrt router

Terminal

**Fig. 3.3** The whole network structure

**Table 3.3** Parameters extracted from different video sites

|  | Youku APP | Web Youku | Potato Video | Iqiyi Video | Tencent Video |
|---|---|---|---|---|---|
| Open the video |  | ✓ |  |  |  |
| Viewing duration | ✓ | ✓ |  |  |  |
| Computer ID | ✓ | ✓ |  |  |  |
| Mobile phone terminal system | ✓ |  |  |  |  |
| Start time of video | ✓ | ✓ |  |  |  |
| End time of video | ✓ |  |  |  |  |
| Video total time | ✓ | ✓ |  |  |  |
| Video frame rate |  | ✓ |  |  |  |
| Video link |  | ✓ |  |  |  |
| Click | ✓ |  |  |  |  |
| Pause |  | ✓ |  |  |  |
| Play |  | ✓ | ✓ | ✓ | ✓ |
| Speed |  | ✓ | ✓ | ✓ | ✓ |
| Back |  | ✓ | ✓ | ✓ | ✓ |
| Switch to HD |  | ✓ | ✓ | ✓ | ✓ |
| Switch to SD |  | ✓ | ✓ | ✓ | ✓ |
| Other resolution conversion |  | ✓ | ✓ | ✓ | ✓ |

It is noted that "open the video" indicates when the user opens the video. "Video start" means the start time of video content playing after pre-launch advertising. The "computer ID" clearly indicates on which computer the video is played.

2. User's identity, habit, and preference gathered by questionnaire

The content of the questionnaire can be roughly divided into three parts:

 (i) User's identity information (including grade, gender, age, etc.).
 (ii) User's habits (including browsing frequency, browsing length, viewing ratio).
(iii) User's self-evaluation (including tolerance time for normal video, tolerance time for video of interest, tolerance for video buffering, general way of viewing video, and evaluation of one's temper).

The reason for the user's identity information gathering is that it can help to understand the user experience when they watch videos. Users from different genders, ages, education levels may have different preference during viewing videos, while users having the same identity information may have similar experience. Due to the limitations of data collection, service data on selected undergraduates and postgraduates from three grades can be concerned. Through analysis, academic and age gaps are not very obvious. However, we can find that there are still some gaps in the behaviors and habits of the students from different grades during viewing videos.

When concerning personality, it can be divided into two parts: user's behavior habits and user's self-evaluation. By examining the user's behavioral habits, it is possible to highlight some content that clearly violates the user's habits. By analyzing the content, it is possible to better identify the factors that affect the user experience.

In summary, the specific questionnaire is shown in Table 3.4 as follows:

**Table 3.4** The meaning of each field in the questionnaire

| Description | Options |
| --- | --- |
| Sex | Male/female |
| Age | Under 16/16–18/19–21/22–24/25–27/over 27 |
| Grade | Undergraduate/postgraduate/Ph.D. candidates |
| Number of days per week | 1–2 days/week / 3–4 days/week / 5–7 days/week/everyday |
| Duration of each visit | Within 1 min/1–3 min/3–5 min/5–10 min/10–30 min/30–60 min/over60 min |
| Length of each video watch | Under 10%/11–20%/21–40%/41–60%/61–80%/81–90%/over90% |
| Ordinary video buffer tolerance | 0–30 s/30 s to 1 min/1–5 min/5–10 min/over 10 min |
| Interested video buffer tolerance | 0–30 s/30 s to 1 min/1–5 min/5–10 min/over 10 min |
| Video advertising tolerance | Under 5 s/5–10 s/10–30 s/30 s to 1 min/1–3 min/more than 3 min |
| Character self-assessment | Very irritable/more irritable/moderate/slow down/very slow |

### 3.1.3  Dataset Crawled Across the Web

Since the data obtained directly from the collection and storage platform only contains the descriptions of video programs, there is no corresponding key data for the specific episode. Therefore, we supplement the data of the collection and storage platform in Sect. 3.1.2 through distributed crawlers, such as episode tag data (episode_tag), video length (video_length), and scoring data (episode_score). In addition, since the danmaku information is a real-time comment posted by the user on the video content, reflecting the actual subjective feeling of the user while viewing the program, we also crawl the corresponding danmaku information.

In summary, we mainly collect the following three aspects of data: episodes information, single episode information, and danmaku information. Considering the scale and crawling content of third-party platforms, we propose the following distributed crawler structure based on scrapy.

As shown in Fig. 3.4, the structure is divided into a master crawler, a drama crawler, a single-set crawler, a danmaku crawler, a key-value storage database, and a relational database. The master crawler is mainly used for performing status monitoring, abnormal alarms, etc. The drama crawler is responsible for extracting episode information from the traversing website page, generating a list of pending singular sets, etc., and then storing them in a key-value database, a relational database, and crawling. At the same time, it generates the episode crawl log. The single-set crawler is responsible for obtaining the URL from the key-value database and crawling the single-set information and storing it in the database, and generating a single-set crawl log. The danmaku crawler is responsible for crawling the user's comment data and parsing it into the relational database and generating the corresponding inbound log.

**Fig. 3.4** Scrapy-based distributed crawler structure

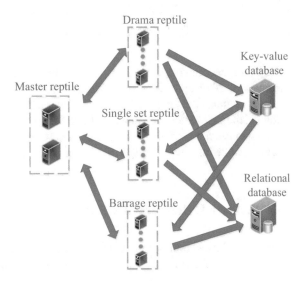

**Table 3.5**  Specific fields of video information

| Field | Meaning |
| --- | --- |
| Danmaku ID | It is used to indicate the latest danmaku file ID corresponding to the program, which helps the player to quickly locate the xml file when loading, usually 8 digits |
| Video ID | Indicates the ID of the video, typically 7 digits |
| Video name | Indicates the name of the episode video, which may not exist, and is usually replaced by the episode name when it does not exist |

**Table 3.6**  Specific fields of user's danmaku data

| Field | Meaning |
| --- | --- |
| Creation time | The time when the user released the danmaku, specifically to the second, such as 2018-1-16 18:30:19.18407. A number of digits are reserved after the decimal point to facilitate video displaying at a uniform time |
| User ID | It is used to identify the information of the user in an encrypted information, such as 1e5a3e6e. It can only be used to find information published by the user in other danmakus |
| Occurrence time | It is used to inform the player when to display the danmaku during playback, which is different from traditional user comments, and can feedback the user's feeling about the video service in real time. It is mainly expressed in seconds, such as 246.485, which means that the time when the danmaku appears in the video is 4 min and 6.485 s |
| Class | The label indicates the class of the danmaku. Danmakus in the ordinary pool is marked as 0, while danmakus in the caption pool is marked as 1 |
| Pattern | It is used to indicate the dynamic effects when the danmaku appears, 3 means rolling danmaku, 4 means bottom danmaku, 5 means top danmaku, 6 means reverse danmaku, 7 means designated position, 8 means arbitrary position |
| Font size | It is used to indicate the size of the fonts in the danmaku |
| Font color | It is used to indicate the color of the fonts in the danmaku |
| Content | It indicates the actual content of the danmaku. It stores the content by UNICODE encoding |

Through the crawler, a total of 45,359,720 user danmaku data, 52,035 video information, 3072 episode information, and 7519 video tag information are collected. It contains the latest 3000 user danmaku data in the videos. The main fields of the video information are shown in Table 3.5.

The specific fields of the user's danmaku data are shown in Table 3.6.

The episode information fields are shown in Table 3.7.

## 3.2  Feature Extraction for Subjective Influencing Factors

Since original data coming from the IPTV and OTT service datasets mainly contain system-related IFs, context-related and user-related IFs/features are needed to be

**Table 3.7**  Specific fields of episode information

| Field | Meaning |
| --- | --- |
| Episode length | Indicate the total length of episodes |
| Episode premiere time | Indicate the first showtime of the episode |
| Episode ID | The full station unique ID used to represent the episode |
| Number of people | Indicate the episode has multiple people put it in a collection for later viewing |
| Number of danmakus | The number of danmakus used to represent all the videos included in the episode |
| Episode tag | Indicate the official classification of episodes |

extracted from original data. In this section, some of our proposed methods for extracting subjective user-related IFs are described, which includes user viewing time ratio calculation, user interest inference, user type classification, user behavior analysis, user comment, and danmaku parsing.

### 3.2.1   User Viewing Time Ratio Calculation

First of all, the popularity of a program can actually be found from the length of viewing time. If the viewing time is long, it means the user prefers the program. Therefore, the viewing time ratio indicator can be selected to measure the user's engagement. The higher the user's engagement is, the better the user's QoE is, and vice versa.

1. Take viewing time ratio as a feature

The user viewing time ratio $V (V \in [0, 1])$ is calculated as follows [1]:

$$V = \frac{T_{end\_time} - T_{start\_time}}{T_{collect\_time} + T - T_{start\_time}}, \tag{3.1}$$

where $T_{collect\_time}$ indicates the collection time of each video viewing record. $T_{start\_time}$ indicates the start time of each video viewing record. $T_{end\_time}$ shows the end time of each video viewing record. The difference between $T_{start\_time}$ and $T_{end\_time}$ is expressed as the duration of the record, that is, the user's viewing time. During the data collection process, the set-top box packs the user's viewing history into a set of records every 300 s and uploads them to the database. $T_{collect\_time}$ is the start time of the first record in a set of records, which is the start time of the record in this group. $T$ represents the packing time of a set of records. In the IPTV service dataset, it is 300 s.

Figure 3.5 is a cumulative distribution function of viewing time ratio. This function can be considered to represent QoE. It can be seen that this is a rising

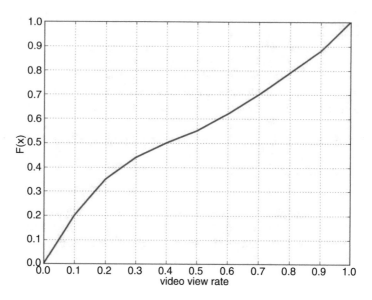

**Fig. 3.5** Cumulative distribution function of viewing time ratio

curve, and about half of the users' viewing time ratio is lower than 0.4. Even the very low user viewing time ratio (less than 0.1) accounts for about 20%.

In order to analyze the influences of various parameters for user viewing time ratios, we use four measurements, Pearson linear correlation, Spearman rank correlation, Kendall rank correlation, and information gain, to describe the relationships between different parameters and user viewing time ratio. From the point of view of the correlation value, these correlation coefficients are very small, which also indicates that the single parameter has little influence on user's viewing time ratio. In other words, user's viewing time ratio is affected by many factors. In the vertical direction, the startup delay, average data rate, video length, and video popularity are negatively correlated with the viewing time ratio. For example, the longer the startup delay is, the lower the viewing time ratio will be, leading to lower QoE. The buffer time and signal length are positively correlated with the viewing time ratio. In the horizontal direction, in general, Spearman rank-related absolute value is larger than the other two values, which is determined by the characteristics of the Spearman rank correlation itself. It is worth noting that in all indicators, the absolute correlation coefficient value of the video length is very large, which means that parameter has a great influence on the viewing rate. The longer the video duration is, the more impatient the user will be, and the viewing time ratio will drop significantly. This also gives us a rough inspiration. While the same content can be expressed, the more streamlined the video is, the more it can cater to the user, so that the user's satisfaction is higher. The whole results are shown in Table 3.8.

In order to avoid calculation problems in which each indicator and the viewing time ratio are not linear, we also use a gain to describe the relationship between

**Table 3.8**  Correlation coefficients and information gain

| | Pearson linear correlation | Spearman rank correlation | Kendall correlation | Information gain |
|---|---|---|---|---|
| Startup delay | −0.03 | −0.17 | −0.11 | 25% |
| Buffer time | 0.02 | 0.05 | 0.03 | 42% |
| Average data transfer rate | −0.05 | −0.07 | −0.05 | 2% |
| Transmission data rate deviation | 0.11 | 0.15 | 0.1 | 13% |
| Signal strength | 0.1 | 0.1 | 0.07 | 26% |
| Video length | −0.15 | −0.45 | −0.31 | 9% |
| Video popularity | −0.14 | −0.12 | −0.08 | 24% |

them. The gains of startup delay and buffer time reach 25% and 42%, respectively, indicating that these two network-related parameters have a great impact on user QoE. The average data transfer rate gain is only 2%, which has little effect. This is because this indicator does not fully represent the transmission throughput. When the packet loss rate increases due to network congestion or other events, even if the transmission data rate is large, throughput is still small and user satisfaction is reduced. The three variance gains in the table are not small. The variance of the transmission data rate represents the stability of the network. The more stable the network, the better the user experience, that is, the better the video QoE. The gains in video length and popularity are still high, indicating that they have a large impact on the user experience. For the Wi-Fi signal strength, as it has a certain impact on the buffer duration, start delay, and the transmission data rate, the degree of influence is between the three, which is also in line with our expectations.

2. User viewing time ratio is more quantitative than MOS value

In addition, viewing time ratio cannot only be used as a feature. When QoE is not obtained through subjective investigation, it can also be represented by quantification of viewing time ratio.

Specifically, when a user watches a program for more than 300 s, a viewing behavior is divided into a plurality of viewing history groups. The viewing time ratio of a user's viewing behavior is the average of multiple records in multiple recording packages. The viewing ratio of a user's viewing session is the average of the proportion of all viewing behaviors contained in the session. For example, a user viewing session is: watch program 1 from 8:31 to 8:32; watch program 2 from 8:32 to 8:40. The viewing session is included in two group records. The first group records the range of 8:30–8:35, which contains two records. Record 1 watches program 1 from 8:31 to 8:32. The viewing ratio is $V = \frac{8:32-8:31}{8:30+5-8:31} = \frac{60 \text{ s}}{240 \text{ s}} = 0.25$. Record 2 watches program 2 from 8:32 to 8:35, and its viewing ratio is $V = \frac{8:35-8:32}{8:30+5-8:32} = \frac{180 \text{ s}}{180 \text{ s}} = 1$. The second set of records has a collection range of 8:35–8:40, and it contains a record that watches program 2 from 8:35 to 8:40 with a viewing ratio of $V = \frac{8:40-8:35}{8:35+5-8:35} = \frac{180 \text{ s}}{180 \text{ s}} = 1$. Therefore, the proportion of program 1 viewing behavior is 0.25. The program 2 viewing behavior is 1, which is

**Table 3.9** Mapping relations
between $V$ and MOS [1]

| $V$ | MOS |
|---|---|
| [0, 0.2) | 1 |
| (0.2, 0.4] | 2 |
| (0.4, 0.6] | 3 |
| (0.6, 0.8] | 4 |
| (0.8, 1] | 5 |

the average of the next two viewing records. After the viewing ratio is calculated, the MOS is mapped as shown in Table 3.9.

### 3.2.2   User Interest Inference

Due to the explosion of video programs, it needs to quickly infer user interest in order to efficiently allocate their interested video programs. Here, we make full use of the proposed user viewing time ratio in Sect. 3.2.1, which measures the subjective viewing experience of users from an objective perspective. Then, considering the current and future interests of users, a combinational latent Dirichlet allocation model is proposed, and the corresponding batch Gibbs sampling algorithm is designed for realizing user interest inference. In addition, considering the real-time processing requirements in the applications, an online Gibbs sampling algorithm for the proposed model is also given [2].

We use part of IPTV service dataset which contains viewing records of 1100 users and 7000 unique TV programs, where different episodes of TV programs are considered as the same program. In addition, all of the viewing records are divided into three types which are Live TV, time-shift TV, and VoD.

In order to realize better accuracy of user interest inference and thus evaluate user QoE, we change the structure of initial LDA model [3]. Figure 3.6 shows probabilistic graphical model representation of the combinational LDA model. In this figure, two branches represent the generation process of two programs whose viewing time ratios are over 20% and 5–20%, respectively.

Specifically, TV programs whose viewing time ratios less than 5% would be cleaned among data preprocessing. On one hand, to improve the accuracy of interest inference, we would make use of records that the user has watched the most of contents. Therefore, the left side of the combinational LDA describes the generation of programs whose viewing time ratios are more than 20%. The variables in this branch are denoted by superscript "$a$." On the other hand, the proposed combinational LDA would be equipped with the ability of discovering and describing user prospective interest. It needs another branch in the model. It plays an important role in adjusting the ratio of the current interest and predicting user interest in the future. Hence, we select some programs that the user increasingly watches in this time as the right branch of the combinational LDA. The variables

**Fig. 3.6** Probabilistic graphical model representation of the combinational LDA [2]

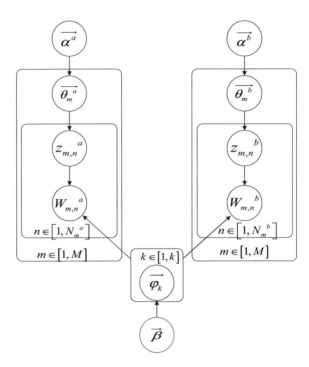

in this branch are denoted by superscript "*b*." In summary, the distributions of programs are generated by these following steps, shown in Fig. 3.6:

1. Two kinds of different distributions of interests are sampled from Dirichlet distribution.
2. For one user, two interests are sampled from multinomial distribution.
3. Both programs are selected from multinomial distribution for two chosen interests.

With the model mentioned above, we can infer the user interest by using batch Gibbs sampling and online Gibbs sampling, respectively.

Figure 3.7 shows the distributions of inferred interests from August 1, 2016, to August 30, 2016, and the user interest distributions from September 3, 2016, to September 12, 2016. From this figure, the distributions of interests generated by the viewing ratio less than 20% play an important role in modeling user prospective interest. Obviously, the viewing records about children's song are increasingly popular during August 1, 2016, to August 30, 2016, which results in more programs of the same interests watched by the user from September 3, 2016, to September 12, 2016, than related programs from August 1, 2016, to August 30, 2016. It has proved that programs with viewing ratios between 5% and 20% could be the key factors to observe user activity and describe user interest in the future. It is reasonable to consider that the combinational LDA model could predict user prospective interest through viewing time ratio by the user.

**Fig. 3.7** Distributions of
interests over time [2]

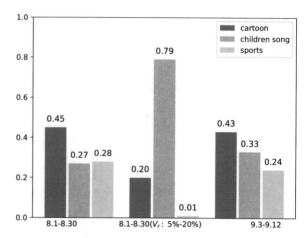

**Fig. 3.8** Precision of userCF,
LDA, and combinational
LDA models [2]

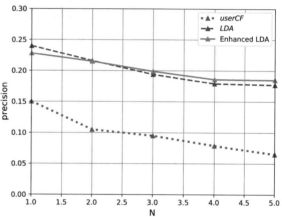

Figure 3.8 shows the precision with the combinational LDA and the competing
LDA and userCF algorithms when they are used for program recommendation. X-
axis indicates the number of recommended programs in the recommendation list.
From these two figures we can see, the userCF has the smallest values of precision
and recall among all models. In other words, comparing with other models, the
performance of userCF algorithm is worse than the LDA and the combinational
LDA algorithms. On account of the sparsity of user-program rating matrix, many
null values lead to low efficiency and accuracy of recommendation. The program
will not be recommended if it is not rated before by the target users or their similar
users. Moreover, userCF wouldn't predict the prospective programs or interests
that the user will watch. LDA model and combinational LDA model recommend
TV programs related to the topics that the user used to be interested in. As the
combinational LDA model filters some useless programs, it improves the accuracy
of recommendation with the increase of the number $N$. When the value of $N$ is
greater than 2, the combinational LDA performs better than the LDA model.

### 3.2.3 User Type Classification

User type is closely related to the user QoE. For example, users with different age groups and habits have different emphasis on the video programs. If user type can be known in advance, QoE evaluation can be performed easily.

Here, we take the user's viewing records as input and use the dynamic time warping (DTW) algorithm to classify the user type. The classified types are elderly users, office young workers, mixed users, and other users.

Firstly, we briefly introduce the principle of DTW. DTW [4] is a technique to obtain the shortest distance of two time series by extending or shortening these series. Specifically, the main principle is to construct a distance matrix between two time series to calculate the dynamic distortion path, and generate a cumulative distance matrix according to the distance matrix to obtain the shortest distance.

Secondly, by analyzing viewing records, we find that viewing time for office workers concentrates on 7–10 pm in weekday. For old users, they view programs between early morning and 9 pm. For the mixed users, the distributions have the characteristics of the above two types. For the other users, the regulations are not obvious.

Finally, based on the above analysis and the principles and characteristics of DTW, we can implement similar user classification based on their viewing time and records. The algorithm is shown as follows:

**Step 1**: Perform user viewing statistics

Since we classify users according to their viewing habits, we firstly count the number of times users watched from 0 am to 11 pm during a month.

**Step 2**: Get viewing trend data for typical users

According to the above statistical results, three representative distribution statistics are obtained associated with three user types. It is noted that each of which uses the average number of views per hour from the selected typical users.

**Step 3**: Calculate the distance matrix $M_n$

The number of views for the $n$th user to be classified is compared with the typical user by calculating the distance matrix $M_n$. The number of rows and columns of the matrix is the length of type viewing times of the target typical user and the length of viewing times of the user to be classified. The values in every element of that matrix are the distance between the above two records of the corresponding position.

**Step 4**: Calculate the cumulative distance matrix $MC_n$

The distance matrix is further manipulated to obtain a cumulative distance matrix, and the value at the first column position of the first row of the accumulation matrix is the distance value between the two data sequences being compared. The cumulative distance matrix is the same as the distance matrix. The calculation rule is: the matrix value is the sum of the distance matrix value at the corresponding position and the smallest cumulative distance matrix value in the left, upper, and upper

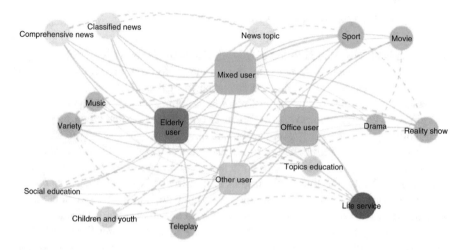

**Fig. 3.9** The classified user type and the associated preference of programs

left positions of the position. The calculation of the cumulative distance matrix is carried out layer by layer, and it is necessary to advance the calculation to the upper right based on the calculated values, and finally obtain the distance between the two sequences. This distance is called the DTW distance, denoted as VAL.

**Step 5**: Obtain the user type

Set the threshold $\theta$. If VAL $>\theta$, it is judged as a mixed user, and vice versa is an elderly user or an office worker. The smaller the VAL value calculated according to the corresponding class, the more similar the user belongs to that category.

Based on the IPTV service dataset, the classified user type and the associated preference of programs after performing the above algorithm are shown in Fig. 3.9.

## 3.2.4 User Behavior Analysis

During the process of viewing videos, users often make pauses or change video resolutions for a better viewing experience. This series of user behavior is a visual reflection of their current choices, often reflecting or even inferring their expectations. Moreover, emotions are one of the intuitive features that reflect the user experience [5]. Based on the IPTV service dataset, the following features are considered and deeply analyzed:

1. Pause behavior

Pause behavior means that the user stops playing the video for a short period of time for some reasons. Based on the reason for the suspension behavior, we further divide this behavior into types of active pause and passive pause. Active pause refers to the pause behavior when playing smooth. In other words, the pause behavior is caused by the user's own reasons. Passive pause refers to the pause behavior caused by waiting for the buffer of the video when the playback is unstable. Therefore, passive pause always causes the user to be dissatisfied with the experience and affects the user QoE.

From the IPTV service dataset, the number of pauses and pause duration are denoted as *pause_num, pause_duration*, and the current network status field, NETWORK_CONDITION, can be represented as *status*, reflecting the network condition when a user is currently viewing the video. That is, whether the video is played smoothly, and the average duration of the pause is calculated as follows:

$$pause\_avg\_duration = \begin{cases} \frac{pause\_duration}{pause\_num}, & status = 1 \\ 0, & status = 0 \end{cases}. \tag{3.2}$$

If the status is 0, it means the network is smooth. The pause behavior does not affect the user QoE. On the contrary, when the status is 1, the network status is poor. The pause behavior affects the user experience.

2. Switch behavior

User switch is also a common type of behavior. For example, the user frequently switches channels during a period of time, and the more the number of handovers, that is, the shorter the time that the user stays on a certain channel, indicating that the user is less interested in the content of the current channel. The success of the handover will also affect the user experience. The more failures are, the lower the user current experience is.

Assume that the number of switch, the number of failed handovers, and the number of successful handovers, respectively, are denoted as *switch_num, switch_failure_num*, and *switch_success_num*. The handover failure ratio and handover success ratio can be defined as:

$$switch\_failure\_rate = \frac{swich\_failure\_num}{switch\_num}, \tag{3.3}$$

$$switch\_success\_rate = \frac{swich\_success\_num}{switch\_num}. \tag{3.4}$$

In addition, switching delays can also affect the user experience. The average delay for each switch is as follows:

$$switch\_avg\_delay = \frac{switch\_delay}{switch\_num}. \tag{3.5}$$

Although each user has different tolerances for the length of the delay and the number of handovers, in general, the more handover failures, the longer the average delay of handover is, leading to worse user experience. From that we can get

$$QoE \sim \frac{1}{switch\_avg\_delay} \tag{3.6}$$

$$QoE \sim \frac{1}{switch\_failure\_rate}. \tag{3.7}$$

3. Quit behavior

The quit behavior means that the user quits when viewing the video. Similar to the pause behavior, this behavior can be divided into active quit and passive quit. Active quit refers to the quit behavior when playback is smooth, while passive quit refers to the exit behavior when playback is unstable. The former is always caused by the user's own reasons, and has nothing to do with the video quality, so it has nothing to do with the QoE evaluation. Passive quit is always due to the user's inability to tolerate these levels of video impairment and may therefore affects QoE assessment.

$$Quit = \begin{cases} 1, & passive\ quit \\ 0, & active\ quit. \end{cases} \tag{3.8}$$

4. Changing video resolution behavior

The choice of video resolution is also one of the common behaviors during video viewing. Changing video resolution means that the user adjusts the quality of the video to a lower or higher level, which reflects the user's desire for video clarity. With the continuous development of video technology, users have higher and higher requirements for video clarity. Users always switch the resolution of a certain video to a higher level, which means that users prefer this type of video. If the user is forced to reduce the clarity of the video for the smoothness of the playback, the QoE will drop, and it is very likely that the video will be abandoned due to the clarity of the video.

### 3.2.5 User Comment & Danmaku Parsing

In terms of video and user interactions, as video websites spring up, users have more and more channels and ways to express their feelings about viewing videos, such as appreciating, thumbs-up, sharing to friends, sending comments, sending danmaku, and other behaviors. Among the numerous behaviors to express users' opinions and feelings, danmaku is more and more popular among the young users. As a new type of comment on video, danmaku has been greatly improved in real-time, social and interactive aspects compared with traditional video comments [6]. Due to the timeliness and interactivity of danmaku, and the trend of gradual promotion to other products, such as games, live sports, online answering questions, etc., the research on danmaku can better understand the reasons for the changes in user instantaneous experience.

The real-time performance of the danmaku is mainly reflected in the timeline and the content of the video. The diversity of the danmaku is mainly reflected in its ability to send colorful bullets depending on the needs of the sender and the permissions. The sociality of the danmaku is mainly reflected in the fact that the user who is viewing later will see the user's danmaku when the front user is viewing the video. When a large number of danmakus appear in a certain scene, the user will have a sense of resonance.

As described above, we have obtained a large amount of video danmaku, video label data, and series information data through distributed crawler, and the extracted information has been introduced in Sect. 3.1.3.

The specific feature extraction steps of danmaku are mainly divided into natural language processing, instantaneous user experience mapping, and temporal sequence feature extraction for instantaneous user experience [7]. Firstly, natural language processing is carried out for users' danmaku content at this moment to mine the main emotions of users' comments. Then, user emotion within this time is mapped into the instantaneous user experience based on time series. Subsequently, time series feature extraction was carried out for the instantaneous user experience at this moment as well as the previous moment. Finally, the required features were obtained for the following QoE modeling and evaluation.

Specifically, during the process of video playing, the set of danmakus issued by users is $C = \{c_1, c_2, \ldots, c_M\}$. The total number of danmakus is $M$. Assume the measurement interval of instantaneous user experience is $N$ seconds, including $T$ time intervals, then the total length of video is $L = N \times T$. Let $q_{tN}$ denote the user experience in time $[t, t + N - 1]$. Let $C_{tN}$ represent the danmaku set within $[t, t + N - 1]$. The instantaneous user experience sequence within playing time $L$ is $Q_N = \{q_{1N}, q_{2N}, \ldots, q_{TN}\}$.

By using short text analysis based on sentiment lexicons, the probability of positive emotion and negative emotion in probability for each danmaku can be obtained. Therefore, the tendency of user experience can be determined by Eq. (3.9).

$$
c_i = \begin{cases} 1, & D > D_0 \\ 0, & -D_0 \leq D \leq D_0 \\ -1, & D < -D_0 \end{cases} \tag{3.9}
$$

where $D = P_{positive} - P_{negative}$. $D_0$ is the corresponding threshold, which needs to be set manually. "1" represents the positive user experience state, "0" represents the neutral user experience state, while "−1" represents the negative user experience state. The instantaneous user experience $q_{tN}$ within the time interval $[t, t + N - 1]$ is determined by the majority of user experience state, as shown in Eq. (3.10):

$$
q_{tN} = \begin{cases} 1 & |C_{tN}|_{max} = 1 \\ 0 & |C_{tN}|_{max} = 0 \\ -1 & |C_{tN}|_{max} = -1 \end{cases}, \tag{3.10}
$$

where $|C_{tN}|_{max}$ refers to majority of user experience state at the interval $[t, t + N - 1]$. When the number of multiple emotional danmakus are the same at a certain moment, the user experience state at the previous moment will be continued. If it is the first interval, the user experience state will be neutral by default. When $M = 0$, that is, when there is no popup screen at this moment, its default state is also neutral user experience state.

After the quantification of user experience state sequence in $T$ intervals $Q_N = \{q_{1N}, q_{2N}, \ldots, q_{TN}\}$ is completed, the instantaneous user experience sequence of video can be obtained. Then, feature extraction can be performed by arithmetical average and exponentially weighted moving average. The calculation of arithmetical average, $Q_{SMA}$, is shown in Eq. (3.11):

$$
Q_{SMA}(t) = \frac{q_{tN} + q_{(t-1)N} + q_{(t-2)N} + \ldots + q_{(t-span+1)N}}{span}, \tag{3.11}
$$

where $span$ represents the manually set window function. When $t - span + 1 \le 0$, $Q_{SMA}(t) = 0$. Through Eq. (3.11), the corresponding time characteristic sequence is obtained $Q_S = \{Q_{SMA}(1), Q_{SMA}(2), \ldots, Q_{SMA}(T)\}$.

When calculating exponential weighted moving average $Q_{EWMA}$, it is shown in Eq. (3.12):

$$
Q_{EWMA}(t) = \alpha \times q_{tN} + (1 - \alpha) \times Q_{EWMA}(t), \tag{3.12}
$$

where $\alpha = \frac{2}{span+1}$. Finally, the corresponding time characteristic sequence $Q_E = \{Q_{EWMA}(1), Q_{EWMA}(2), \ldots, Q_{EWMA}(T)\}$ can be obtained.

## 3.3  Summary

In this chapter, we introduce details of three datasets collected for multimedia QoE evaluation. Moreover, we focus on the preprocessing and extraction methods for IFs of the QoE, especially user-related IFs. It contains user viewing time ratio calculation, user interest inference, user type classification, user behavior analysis, and user comment and danmaku parsing. These subjective and abstract IFs will further promote multimedia QoE evaluation performance after combined with modeling and prediction described in the subsequent chapter.

# References

1. Huang R, Wei X, Gao Y, Lv C, Mao J, Bao Q (2018) Data-driven QoE prediction for IPTV service. Comput Commun 118(12):195–204
2. Gao Y, Wei X, Zhang X, Zhuang W (2018) A combinational LDA-based topic model for user interest inference of energy efficient IPTV service in smart building. IEEE Access 6:48921–48933
3. Zhang Y, Chen W, Zha H, Gu X (2015) A time-topic coupled LDA model for IPTV user behaviors. IEEE Trans Broadcast 61(1):51–65
4. Kate RJ (2016) Using dynamic time warping distances as features for improved time series classification. Data Min Knowl Disc 30(2):283–312
5. Hao Y, Yang J, Chen M (2019) Emotion-aware video QoE assessment via transfer learning. IEEE Multimed 26(1):31–40
6. Chen Y, Gao Q, Rau P-LP (2017) Watching a movie alone yet together: understanding reasons for watching danmaku videos. Int J Hum Comput Interact 33(9):731–743
7. Huang R (2018) Research on the theory and application of the key technologies of user quality of experience video service. Doctor Thesis, Nanjing University of Posts and Telecommunications (Supervisor: Zhu H, Zhou L)

# Chapter 4
# Multimedia QoE Modeling and Prediction

**Abstract** In this chapter, we focus on our research of multimedia QoE modeling and prediction. Firstly, we introduce two designed multimedia user complaint prediction algorithms: GMM-based oversampling algorithm and decision tree-based cost-sensitive algorithm. Subsequently, we discuss the proposed multimedia QoE modeling and prediction algorithms which are based on artificial neural network (ANN) and long short-term memory (LSTM), respectively. Finally, we briefly describe the newly established multimedia QoE modeling and prediction based on broad learning system (BLS).

## 4.1 Multimedia User Complaint Prediction for Imbalanced Dataset

As described in Sect. 3.1.1, in the IPTV service dataset, the number of user complaint (low QoE) seldom happens compared with non-complaints (high QoE), making the collected dataset imbalanced. Traditional machine learning algorithms cannot handle this issue. Methods adopted to process the imbalanced dataset can be categorized into two main types: sampling-based methods by reconstructing the distributions of dataset from imbalanced into balanced and cost-sensitive based algorithms by changing the costs of misclassified minority examples. In this section, we propose two algorithms belonging to the above two types.

### 4.1.1 GMM-Based Oversampling Algorithm

To make the dataset balanced, the minority samples can be oversampled. When concerning existing works, the synthetic minority oversampling technique (SMOTE) algorithm is an oversampling method proposed to overcome the shortcomings of random oversampling. The SMOTE produces the same number of sample points for a single minority sample point. The algorithm does not consider the distance relationships between sample points, which increases the overlap of majority and

X. Wei, L. Zhou, *Multimedia QoE Evaluation*, SpringerBriefs in Computer Science,
https://doi.org/10.1007/978-3-030-23350-1_4

minority classes to some extent. To this end, an adaptive oversampling algorithm generated for sample point distances is proposed to overcome this drawback. The current representative algorithms are borderline-SMOTE (BSMOTE) and adaptive synthetic sampling (ADASYN) approaches [1]. The BSMOTE algorithm primarily produces the same number of sample points for a few class boundary sample points. The ADASYN algorithm generates different numbers of sampling points according to the distribution of a few types of samples in the BSMOTE algorithm.

The BSMOTE and ADASYN algorithms handle imbalanced dataset by generating new minority class samples directly from existing samples. They don't grasp the property of the minority class samples. If we can effectively grasp the distribution of minority class samples, the generated new samples will be more representative and can more appropriately describe the property of minority class. It may finally be convenient for the subsequent classifiers to predict user's complaint. Mixture model is a kind of statistical tool for modeling probability distribution of real datasets. Due to its benefits from analytical tractability and universal approximation capacity for continuous probability density functions, it has been widely used in several domains [2, 3].

Based on the above analysis and motivation, different from the traditional oversampling algorithms, we use Gaussian mixture model (GMM) to describe the distributions of the minority class samples. Then, we can use the constructed GMM to generate new minority class samples. After performing the proposed estimation and generation algorithms, the property of original minority class samples is learned and the new minority class samples can be obtained, changing the dataset from imbalanced to balanced. Finally, traditional classification algorithm is used to process the balanced dataset, finishing training and prediction of user complaint tasks.

The steps of our proposed GMM-based oversampling algorithm are described as follows [4]:

**Step 1**:    Select GMM for describing distribution of minority class samples

Assume the dataset is denoted as $D = \{(\mathbf{x}_i, y_i)\}, i = 1, \ldots, N$, where $N$ is the number of samples. Let $\mathbf{x}_i$ denote input, output $y_i \in Y = \{-1, 1\}$. Moreover, let $D_{maj} \subset D$ and $D_{min} \subset D$ denote majority and minority sample set, respectively. The relationship of these two sets are $D_{maj} \cap D_{min} = \{\emptyset\}$ and $D_{maj} \cup D_{min} = D$.

Firstly, we select GMM to describe the distribution of minority samples $\mathbf{x}_i^{min} \in D_{min}, i = 1, \ldots, N_{min}$. As GMM can be seen as a linear superposition of multiple Gaussian components, it has the ability of approaching arbitrary distribution. The probability density function of the GMM can be expressed by

$$p(\mathbf{x}_i^{min}) = \sum_{k=1}^{K} p(z_i = k) p(\mathbf{x}_i^{min} | z_i = k) = \sum_{k=1}^{K} \pi_k N(\mathbf{x}_i^{min} | \mu_k, \Sigma_k), \qquad (4.1)$$

where $z_i$ is a random binary variable which is a 1-of-$K$ representation. $z_i = k$ denotes $\mathbf{x}_i^{min}$ coming from the $k$th component. $\{\mu_k, \Sigma_k, \pi_k\}$ are expectation, covariance, and weight of the $k$th component, respectively. $\pi_k$ satisfies the condition: $0 \leq \pi_k \leq 1$, $\sum_{k=1}^{K} \pi_k = 1$. Finally, the log-likelihood function of GMM when modeling $\mathbf{x}_i^{min} \in D_{min}, i = 1, \dots, N_{min}$, is shown in

$$\log p(D_{min}) = \sum_{i=1}^{N_{min}} \ln \left\{ \sum_{k=1}^{K} \pi_k N(\mathbf{x}_i^{min} | \mu_k, \Sigma_k) \right\}. \tag{4.2}$$

**Step 2:** Estimate parameters in GMM from the original minority class samples

After modeling distribution of $\mathbf{x}_i^{min} \in D_{min}, i = 1, \dots, N_{min}$, the next step is to estimate parameters of GMM. A good tool for maximum likelihood estimation of mixed models is the expectation maximization (EM) algorithm. It is an iterative algorithm for maximum likelihood estimation when the observed data are incomplete data, which greatly reduces the computational complexity of maximum likelihood estimation.

Based on the EM algorithm, conditional distribution $p(z_i | \mathbf{x}_i^{min})$ should be given first in the E-step, which is

$$\gamma(i, k) = \frac{p(z_i = k) p(\mathbf{x}_i^{min} | z_i = k)}{\sum_{k'=1}^{K} p(z_i = k') p(\mathbf{x}_i^{min} | z_i = k')},$$

$$= \frac{\pi_k N(\mathbf{x}_i^{min} | \mu_k, \Sigma_k)}{\sum_{k'=1}^{K} \pi_k' N(\mathbf{x}_i^{min} | \mu_k', \Sigma_k')}. \tag{4.3}$$

It is noted that $\gamma(i, k)$ can be seen as the probability of data $\mathbf{x}_i^{min}$ in the $k$th component. After obtaining $\gamma(i, k)$, in the subsequent M-step, parameters in the GMM can be derived, which are

$$\pi_k = \frac{N_k}{N_{min}},$$

$$\mu_k = \frac{1}{N_k} \sum_{i=1}^{N_{min}} \gamma(i, k) \mathbf{x}_i^{min},$$

$$\Sigma_k = \frac{1}{N_k} \sum_{i=1}^{N_{min}} \gamma(i, k) (\mathbf{x}_i^{min} - \mu_k)(\mathbf{x}_i^{min} - \mu_k)^{\mathrm{T}}, \tag{4.4}$$

where $N_k = \sum_{i=1}^{N_{min}} \gamma(i, k)$, which means the number of data $\mathbf{x}_i^{min}$ assigned to the $k$th component.

Repeat E-step and M-step until the log-likelihood function $\log p(D_{min})$ converges. The output of this step is the estimated parameters of GMM, $\{\pi_k, \mu_k, \Sigma_k\}_{k=1}^{K}$.

**Step 3**:    Generate new minority class samples by the learned GMM

After the GMM estimation procedure is finished, it can be considered that the distribution property of the minority class samples can be grasped and represented by this learned model. Then, new minority class samples can be generated by the learned GMM.

Firstly, a random number $\delta$ in $[0, 1]$ is uniformed generated. Then, if $\delta \in \left[ \sum_{c=1}^{k-1} \pi_c, \sum_{c=1}^{k} \pi_c \right]$, a new minority sample is generated from Gaussian distribution,

$$\tilde{\mathbf{x}}_i^{min} \sim N(\mu_k, \Sigma_k), \quad i = 1, \ldots, \tilde{N}_{min}, \tag{4.5}$$

where $\tilde{\mathbf{x}}_i^{min} \in \tilde{D}_{min}$. $\tilde{N}_{min}$ denotes the number of new minority class samples needing to be generated, which is determined by the imbalanced dataset. In other words, the above generation process needs to be repeated $\tilde{N}_{min}$ times. The final minority class set is $D_{min}^{new} = D_{min} + \tilde{D}_{min}$, which is used for the following classification algorithms, such as Naive Bayes, SVM, etc.

## 4.1.2  Decision Tree-Based Cost-Sensitive Algorithm

In this subsection, we solve the multimedia user complaint prediction problem by cost-sensitive based algorithm. Specifically, we propose an improved decision tree model to deal with the imbalance dataset.

The building procedure of the model is shown in Fig. 4.1.

1. CART model

CART is one kind of representative machine learning algorithms [6]. The idea is to construct a binary decision tree based on the training dataset through iterative analysis. CART algorithm uses the Gini Index as the criteria to choose the best characteristic variables. Gini Index is defined as follows:

$$Gini(D) = 1 - \sum_{k=1}^{K} \left( \frac{|C_k|}{|D|} \right)^2, \tag{4.6}$$

where $D$ is the training dataset; $|D|$ is the number of the training dataset; $k$ is the number of classes; $C_k (k = 1, 2, \ldots, K)$ is a class; $|C_k|$ is the number of instances belonging to the class $C_k$.

If the training dataset $D$ is divided into two parts $D_1$ and $D_2$ by the value of $a$ which belongs to the characteristic $A$, Gini Index of the training dataset $D$ with the characteristic $A$ is

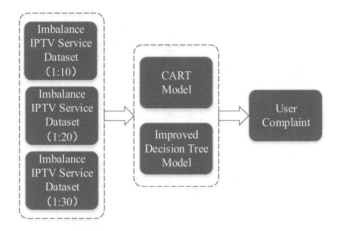

**Fig. 4.1** Procedure of the decision tree-based cost-sensitive algorithm [5]

$$Gini(D, A) = \frac{|D_1|}{|D|} Gini(D_1) + \frac{|D_2|}{|D|} Gini(D_2). \tag{4.7}$$

As we all know, Gini Index needs to be as small as possible. The CART algorithm is summarized as follows:

**Step 1**:  Calculate Gini Index of the training dataset with all characteristics. The training dataset $D$ is divided into two parts $D_1$ and $D_2$ by the value of $a$, which belongs to the characteristic $A$. According to Eq. (4.7), calculate Gini Index when $A = a$.

**Step 2**:  Choose the optimal characteristic and split point to make Gini Index of the dataset smallest. According to the optimal characteristic and split point, split the dataset into two child nodes.

**Step 3**:  Two child nodes recursively call Step 1 and Step 2.

**Step 4**:  Return the CART classification tree.
    The disadvantage of CART model is that it is unstable. It will create biased trees if some classes dominate. So we proposed improved decision tree model. It has a good prediction in the imbalance dataset.

2. Decision tree-based cost-sensitive algorithm

Before the introduction of the decision tree-based cost-sensitive algorithm, we first introduce several performance indicators of the imbalanced dataset using classification models. In the binary classification problem, indicators for evaluation can be defined based on confusion matrix, shown in Table 4.1.

Based on the above table, accuracy, precision, recall, F-measure, and G-mean are defined as follows:

**Table 4.1** Confusion matrix for performance evaluation [7]

|                             | True condition positive | True condition negative |
| --------------------------- | ----------------------- | ----------------------- |
| Predicted condition positive | True positive (TP)      | False positive (FP)     |
| Predicted condition negative | False negative (FN)     | True negative (TN)      |

$$Accuracy = \frac{TP + TN}{P + N},$$

$$Precision = \frac{TP}{TP + FP},$$

$$Recall = \frac{TP}{TP + FN},$$

$$F\text{-}measure = \frac{(1 + \beta)^2 \times Recall \times Precision}{\beta^2 \times Recall + Precision},$$

$$G\text{-}mean = \sqrt{\frac{TP}{TP + FN} \times \frac{TN}{TN + FP}}. \tag{4.8}$$

Importantly, here we modify F-measure in Eq. (4.8):

$$F(\alpha) = \frac{Recall \times Precision}{Recall + Precision + \alpha}. \tag{4.9}$$

After the above descriptions, the decision tree-based cost-sensitive algorithm is proposed [5]. There are two different changes between decision tree-based cost-sensitive algorithm and CART. Firstly, we apply $F(\alpha)$ to our improved decision tree model. Specifically, the improved decision tree model uses $F(\alpha)$ as the criteria to choose the best characteristic variables. $F(\alpha)$ needs to be as large as possible. It can create healthy trees when the dataset is imbalanced.

Secondly, traditional decision tree chooses the class in the leaf node by majority rule, which may create biased trees. As the minority class is important, we propose the conditional minority rule. When the number of minority class in the leaf node is larger than the threshold we set, we determine the leaf node belongs to the minority class. When the number of minority class in leaf nodes is smaller than the threshold we set, we use traditional majority rule to determine the class of the leaf node. The threshold is defined as:

$$threshold = S \times \gamma, \tag{4.10}$$

where $S$ is the number of the minority class in the imbalance dataset; $0 \le \gamma \le 1$. Finally, the improved decision tree algorithm is summarized as follows:

**Step 1**:   Calculate the threshold of leaf nodes by Eq. (4.10).
**Step 2**:   Divide the training dataset $D$ into two parts $D_1$ and $D_2$ by the value of $a$ which belongs to the characteristic $A$. According to Eq. (4.9), calculate $F(\alpha)$.
**Step 3**:   Choose the optimal characteristic and split point to make $F(\alpha)$ of the dataset largest. According to the optimal characteristic and split point, split the dataset into two child nodes.
**Step 4**:   When the child node is the leaf node, we calculate the number of the minority class in the leaf node. If the number of the minority class in the leaf node is larger than the threshold, we use the conditional minority rule. Otherwise, we use the traditional majority rule.
**Step 5**:   Two children nodes recursively call Step 2 to Step 4.
**Step 6**:   Output the improved decision tree.

## 4.2   Multimedia QoE Modeling and Prediction Based on Neural Networks

In this section, we introduce two neural networks to build QoE model and realize QoE prediction: one is the artificial neural network (ANN) and the other is the long short-term memory (LSTM) network.

### 4.2.1   Artificial Neural Networks (ANN)

Firstly, we propose an artificial neural network (ANN) to model the relationship between QoE and its IFs when users view TV channels [8]. When concerning IFs, network indicators are used to represent objective IFs. Moreover, user interest indicators *uindex* is also adopted to represent subjective IFs. We split the proposed personal QoE model into three main steps as shown in Fig. 4.2.

When user starts to view TV channels, user interest model is performed to generate user interest list. Then, *uindex* is obtained to measure the user interest in the program. Subsequently, the ANN is chosen and the associated parameters are trained by user interest indicators and network indicators. Further details of this method are described as follows:

**Fig. 4.2**  Flow chart of QoE modeling and prediction based on ANN [8]

**Step 1**:   Generate user interest list

In order to study user interest quantitatively, we firstly build user interest model to generate user interest list. In this process, whether the user is a regular user or new comer is decided by searching view history with user id. If it is the first day for a user enjoying the multimedia service, the model takes the user as new comer. In order to generate user interest list with relevance and diversity, the model generates the user interest list with the user interest program in history. The model also generates public user interest list for new comer with top 10 channels from all users in previous day. Moreover, the model also generates personal interest list for regular users with top 10 from the viewing history in the previous day which maintains the personalization and reflects the variation of user interest. In this step, regular users get his or her own personal user interest list and the list will change in next day according to the viewing history of the day. The new comers get the same public user interest list with top 10 channels from all users in previous day.

**Step 2**:   Get user interest index

We can see that most users have their individual interest in channel and it is hard for the user to change his or her preferences in short time. As each user watches less than 10 channels in Live TV, user interest list which contains popular top 10 channels in previous day can represent that user interest in Live TV in 1 day. *uindex* is proposed to measure and quantify the user interest in specific channel by ratio between viewing time of specific channel and viewing time of all channel in the user interest list. Based on this, we define *uindex* as follows:

$$uindex = \begin{cases} \frac{V_{time}}{V_{sum}}, & channel_{id} \in user_{list} \\ 0, & channel_{id} \notin user_{list} \end{cases}, \tag{4.11}$$

where $V_{time}$ means the sum of the user's viewing time of the channel in previous day. $V_{sum}$ denotes the sum of user's viewing time for all channels in the user interest list in previous day. Each channel from user interest list gets its own *uindex*. If the user spends more time on the channel, *uindex* of the channel will increase due to the viewing time of the channel. If the channel id is not found in user interest list, *uindex* is 0.

**Step 3**:   Train personal QoE model based on ANN

ANN is one of the most popular neural networks for acceptable computational complexity. The theory is based on gradient descent method to iteratively compute gradients for each layer. The basic equation of ANN algorithm is

$$W(n) = W(n) - \triangle W(n),$$

$$\triangle W(n) = \eta \frac{\partial E}{\partial W}(n-1) + \alpha \triangle W(n-1), \tag{4.12}$$

where $W(n)$ means weight at the $n$th iteration, $\triangle W(n)$ means gradient, $\eta$ denotes learning rate and controls the step, $E$ means gradient of error function. It is noted

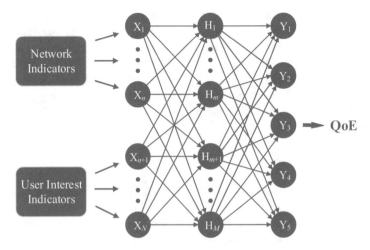

**Fig. 4.3** The structure of the proposed ANN neural network for QoE prediction [8]

that the ANN updates $\eta$ according to each sample rather than all the samples, which in some ways accelerates the speed of finding the optimal solutions. By adapting $\eta$, the parameters in this model can be estimated. Moreover, it is noted that the error function used in this model is

$$E = \frac{1}{|\mathbf{X}|} \sum_{\mathbf{X}} \|y(\mathbf{X}) - \text{ANN}(\mathbf{X})\|^2. \tag{4.13}$$

This ANN consists of three layers named input, hidden, output layers, respectively, shown in Fig. 4.3. $\{X_1, \ldots, X_n\}$ are input neurons. $\{H_1, \ldots, H_m\}$ are hidden neurons. The network has five output nodes $\{Y_1, \ldots, Y_5\}$ to represent QoE which is $\{1, 2, 3, 4, 5\}$ in MOS. The input signal acts on output node through hidden point and gets the output signal by nonlinear transformation. The typical QoE model based on ANN is to find the smallest output error for the dataset by adjusting the weight between hidden and input nodes and threshold. We train hyper-parameters in ANN model and find best choice for building QoE model.

**Step 4**:   Predict QoE for new input data by the trained ANN.


### 4.2.2   LSTM-Attention Model

1. LSTM cell

Recurrent neural network (RNN) is a representative deep learning network. This neural network performs successfully in some domain, such as machine translation and speech recognition. However, theoretical and empirical evidence show that, due to the problem of vanishing gradient descent, RNN shows low performance in training. It cannot remember inputs for a long time. To handle this issue, long short-term memory (LSTM) network using special remember cell to substitute hidden units is proposed. Its natural character is to capture dependency between inputs and outputs. Therefore, the LSTM neural network can learn long-term dependency. A LSTM cell is shown in Fig. 4.4. It has three gates, namely forget gate, input gate, and output gate, to protect and control the cell state. Among them, forget gate is used to decide which information will be thrown away from the cell state. The expression of the forget gate is

$$f_t = \sigma(W_{f_1} \cdot h_{t-1} + W_{f_2} \cdot x_t + b_f), \qquad (4.14)$$

where $W_{f_i}$ and $b_f$ are the weights and bias. $\sigma(\cdot)$ is the sigmoid function. The output of this sigmoid function is between 0 and 1.

The input gate decides which values to update and a *tanh* creates a vector of new values added to the state, shown by Eq. (4.15)

$$i_t = \sigma(W_{i_1} \cdot h_{t-1} + W_{i_2} \cdot x_t + b_i),$$
$$\tilde{C}_t = \tanh(W_{C_1} \cdot h_{t-1} + W_{C_2} \cdot x_t + b_C), \qquad (4.15)$$

According to Eqs. (4.14) and (4.15), it can obtain

$$C_t = f_t \cdot C_{t-1} + i_t \cdot \tilde{C}_t, \qquad (4.16)$$

Moreover, the output gate is

$$o_t = \sigma(W_{o_1} \cdot h_{t-1} + W_{o_2} \cdot x_t + b_o). \qquad (4.17)$$

Finally, the output of this model is

$$h_t = o_t \cdot \tanh(C_t). \qquad (4.18)$$

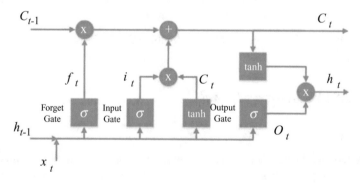

**Fig. 4.4** The structure of the LSTM cell [9]

2. Attention mechanism

In terms of time series and machine translation problems, the model of the encoder–decoder structure of RNN, LSTM has achieved excellent results. However, recurrent models typically computes along the symbol positions of the input and output sequences. Aligning the positions to steps in computation time, they generate a sequence of hidden states $h_t$, as a function of the previous hidden state $h_{t-1}$ and the input for position $t$. This inherently sequential nature precludes parallelization within training examples, which becomes critical at longer sequence lengths, as memory constraints limit batching across examples. Despite achieving higher performance compared to purely statistical methods, the RNN-based and LSTM-based architectures suffer from two serious drawbacks. Firstly, RNN is forgetful, meaning that old information gets washed out after being propagated over multiple time steps. Secondly, there is no explicit word alignment during decoding and therefore the focus is scattered across the entire sequence. Aiming to resolve the issues above, attention mechanism is introduced into neural machine translation [10]. The core of the attention mechanism is to calculate the attention score, described as follows:

**Step 1**: Compute the attention scores: $e_i = a(\mu, v_i)$.
**Step 2**: Perform normalization: $\alpha_i = \exp(e_i) / \sum_{i'} \exp(e_{i'})$.
**Step 3**: Finish encoding: $c = \sum_i \alpha_i v_i$.

In the above steps, $\mu \in R^{d_u}$ is a task-specific pattern vector to match with each element in the sequence $\{v_i\}$ based on the alignment function $a(\mu, v_i)$ that outputs a scalar score $e_i \in R$ to indicate quality of match.

Attention mechanism has become an integral part of compelling sequence modeling and transduction models in various tasks, allowing modeling of dependencies without regard to their distance in the input or output sequences. In all but a few cases, however, such attention mechanism is used in conjunction with a recurrent network.

Attention mechanism can also be considered as a measure of similarity. The more similar the current input is to the target, the greater the weight given to it, indicating that the current output is more dependent on the current input. The attention mechanism has been successfully applied in many research work, especially in the machine translation task.

An attention function can be described as mapping a query and a set of key-value pairs to an output, where the query, keys, values, and output are all vectors. The output is computed as a weighted sum of the values, where the weight assigned to each value is computed by a compatibility function of the query with the corresponding key. As shown in Eqs. (4.19) and (4.20), the scaled dot-product attention and multi-head attention are adopted here.

$$Attention(Q, K, V) = softmax(\frac{QK^T}{\sqrt{d_k}}), \qquad (4.19)$$

$$MultiHead(Q, K, V) = concat(head_1, head_2, \ldots, head_h)W^o,$$

$$head_i = Attention(QW_i^Q, KW_i^K, VW_i^V). \tag{4.20}$$

3. LSTM-Attention algorithm [11]

From the above analysis, the attention mechanism is based on the idea of weights. By introducing new weight information, the relationship between the current output and the previous input is strengthened, thereby optimizing the model and improving the performance of the model.

As is known to all, user QoE has long-term and short-term dependency characteristics, and user QoE at the next moment may be related to QoE of the previous moments. Moreover, user QoE of the current moment may also affect QoE at the next moment. Based on the LSTM model, we introduce the attention mechanism and propose the LSTM-Attention neural network. The network structure diagram is shown in Fig. 4.5. The model introduces the attention mechanism based on LSTM neural network structure to strengthen the user QoE state before and after the connection, thereby improving the performance of the user QoE prediction. In addition, using the bidirectional LSTM neural network, the input data can be

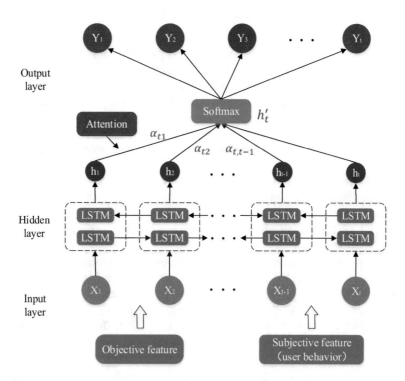

**Fig. 4.5** The structure of the proposed LSTM-Attention neural network for QoE prediction

trained from both forward and backward directions, which can effectively improve the performance of the model.

As shown in Fig. 4.5, the objective feature and user behavior feature obtained in Chap. 3 are used as input data of the model. The input dataset is divided into a training dataset and a test dataset by the proportion of 7:3. Assuming that QoE training dataset is $D = \{(\mathbf{x}_1, y_1), (\mathbf{x}_2, y_2), \ldots, (\mathbf{x}_n, y_n)\}$. The input data $\mathbf{x}_n$ contains $d$ attributes, that is, $\mathbf{x}_n = (x_{n1}, x_{n2}, \ldots, x_{nd})$. The output is MOS value, that is, $y_n = (1, 2, 3, 4, 5)$.

In Fig. 4.5, assume that $h_i$ is the hidden layer state of the bidirectional LSTM output at time $i$. The bidirectional LSTM includes a forward LSTM and a reverse LSTM. The forward LSTM calculates the input timing sequence data $\mathbf{x}_1 \sim \mathbf{x}_t$ to obtain the corresponding timing forward hidden layer state ($\overrightarrow{h}_1, \overrightarrow{h}_2, \ldots, \overrightarrow{h}_t$), while the reverse LSTM will read as input the time series data in reverse, that is, $\mathbf{x}_t \sim \mathbf{x}_1$. For the reverse LSTM, the corresponding hidden layer state ($\overleftarrow{h}_1, \overleftarrow{h}_2, \ldots, \overleftarrow{h}_t$) is obtained, combined with the positive moment of the $i - th$ moment. The hidden state $h_i$ at the $i - th$ moment of the bidirectional LSTM contains the forward state $\overrightarrow{h}_i$ and the reverse hidden state $\overleftarrow{h}_i$, $h_i = [\overrightarrow{h}_i; \overleftarrow{h}_i]^t$.

As we know, QoE prediction depends on their historical experience. In the LSTM neural network, the user QoE at time $t$ (set as $y_t$) is related to the input $\mathbf{x}_1 \sim \mathbf{x}_{t-1}$ of the first $t - 1$ time, and $y_t$ is calculated by the hidden state $h_t$ of the output of the LSTM at time $t$. It is obtained that the hidden state $h_t$ is associated with the hidden state $h_{t-1}$ of the previous moment, and so on. However, if only the output $y_t$ of the current user QoE is directly corresponding to $h_t$, and the hidden state $h_1 \sim h_{t-1}$ which including the historical user QoE information is ignored, some historical user QoE information is obviously ignored. Therefore, we propose the LSTM-Attention model, introducing a variable $c_t$ containing the user context to implement the user's current QoE prediction. The variable $c_t$ is calculated as follows:

**Step 1:** Calculate the attention score $\alpha_{ti}$ of each historical hidden layer state at the current moment according to the hidden layer state $h_i (i = 1, 2, \ldots, t-1)$ before the current time,

$$\alpha_{ti} = W_\alpha \cdot h_i + b_\alpha, \tag{4.21}$$

where $W_\alpha$ is the weight and $b_\alpha$ is the bias, which are obtained by learning in the model training process.

**Step 2:** Standardize the attention score $\overline{\alpha}_{ti}$, $\overline{\alpha}_{ti} = \text{softmax}(\alpha_{ti})$.

**Step 3:** Calculate the variable $c_t$ containing context relationship for user QoE, $c_t = \sum_{i=1}^{t-1} \alpha_{ti} \cdot h_i$.

Combining $c_t$ with the current hidden layer state $h_t$, the new hidden state $h_t'$ is obtained after introducing the attention mechanism at time $t$ is $h_t' = \tanh(W_c \cdot [c_t; h_t])$.

**Step 4:** Obtain the output $y_t$, $y_t = \text{softmax}(W \cdot h_t' + b)$.

The training and prediction process of the proposed LSTM-Attention model are shown in Fig. 4.6.

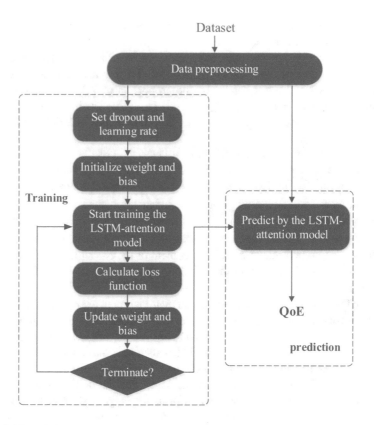

**Fig. 4.6** The training and prediction process of the proposed LSTM-Attention model

In order to verify the applicability and effectiveness of the proposed LSTM model and LSTM-Attention model, we use the IPTV service dataset in Sect. 3.1.1. After data preprocessing and feature extraction in Chap. 3, 70% of the data is used as the training dataset, while the remaining 30% is used for prediction. The nature of user QoE prediction here is actually a typical multi-classification problem.

Based on the long-term and short-term dependences of user history QoE state, the LSTM network is used for QoE prediction. Firstly, we compare the performance of the LSTM model with typical machine learning methods, such as SVM and DT. In addition, in order to prove that the LSTM network has higher learning performance than other machine learning methods, we consider a conventional neural network (NN), which consists of "input-hidden-output" layer structure. Different from NN, the hidden layer of the LSTM is composed of LSTM neurons. In the experimental process, by adjusting the relevant parameters, including selecting the appropriate activation function, different types of optimization algorithms are used. The learning rate of different algorithms is tried to make the model more effective and improve

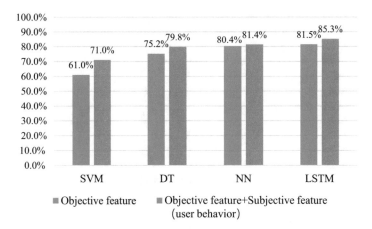

**Fig. 4.7**   QoE prediction accuracy results by four competing models

the accuracy of model classification. At the same time, in order to verify the beneficial of performance after considering user subjective behavior characteristics in Sect. 3.2.4, we compare the prediction model by using two different input datasets. Dataset 1 contains only objective features, while dataset 2 contains both objective and behavior characteristics. The accuracy of the four algorithms for QoE prediction is shown in Fig. 4.7.

As shown in Fig. 4.7, by comparing the accuracy of SVM, DT, NN, and LSTM network with respect to QoE prediction, it is obvious that the performance of the LSTM network model is the best, and the prediction accuracy is 85.3%. For user QoE prediction problem, the user behavior feature extracted in this section affects and effectively improves the performance of the model.

Then, based on the LSTM model, we also evaluate the performance of the attention mechanism, calculate the attention score $\alpha_{ti}$, and propose the LSTM-Attention model. To verify the performance of the LSTM-Attention model, we firstly compare the performance of the LSTM-Attention model with the LSTM model. Since the LSTM-Attention model uses a bidirectional LSTM network structure, in order to compare the performance of the algorithm fairly, the proposed model is also compared with the bidirectional LSTM model without attention mechanism. The experimental results are shown in Fig. 4.8.

As shown in Fig. 4.8, for the objective feature dataset, the LSTM-Attention model is 1.3% more accurate than the one-way LSTM model and 1% more than the two-way LSTM model. For the dataset including objective feature data and behavior characteristics, the performance of the LSTM-Attention model has been significantly improved. The accuracy is 7.8% higher than that of the original LSTM model and 6% higher than the bidirectional LSTM model.

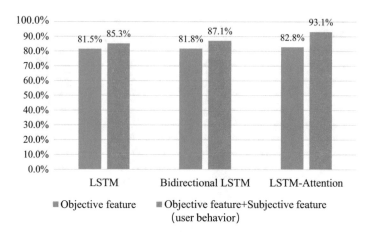

**Fig. 4.8** QoE prediction accuracy results by four LSTM, bidirectional LSTM, and LSTM-Attention models

Finally, the following conclusions can be drawn:

1. User behavior characteristics proposed in Chap. 3 are indeed important factors influencing user QoE. Adding user behavior characteristics in the model can effectively improve the accuracy of QoE prediction.
2. The LSTM-Attention model can further improve the performance of QoE prediction on the basis of the LSTM.

## 4.3   Multimedia QoE Modeling and Prediction Based on Broad Learning System

In this section, we introduce another approach for QoE modeling and prediction. As we all know, deep structure and learning suffer from a time-consuming training process because of a large number of connecting parameters in filters and layers. Moreover, deep neural network model encounters a complete retraining process if the structure is not sufficient to model the system. As a result, the broad learning system (BLS) firstly proposed by Chen is used to offer an alternative way of learning in deep structure [12]. BLS is derived from the traditional random vector functional-link neural network (RVFLNN). Unlike the RVFLNN that takes the input directly and establishes the enhancement nodes, in the BLS, the inputs are firstly mapped to construct a set of mapped features. In addition, the incremental learning algorithm is adopted to update the system dynamically. Specifically, there are only three layers in the BLS. Firstly, raw data $\mathbf{X}$ are transferred and placed as "mapped features" in feature nodes $\mathbf{Z}$. Then, the features are further enhanced to form "enhancement nodes" $\mathbf{H}$. Finally, the connections of all the mapped features and the enhancement

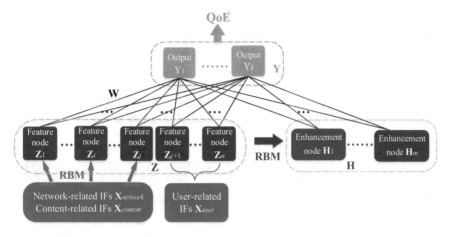

**Fig. 4.9**  The structure of the BLS for multimedia QoE evaluation

nodes are fed into the output **Y**. Ridge regression of the pseudoinverse is designed to find the desired connection weights **W**. It is noted that the BLS can be further simplified by using low-rank approximation, which is considered as an effective tool for processing high-dimensional and large-scale data. The main advantages of the BLS embody in two aspects. Firstly, the computation complexity and time can be substantially reduced when compared with the DL systems under the premise of guaranteeing performance. Secondly, the incremental learning algorithms are performed for fast remodeling in broad expansion without a retraining process if the model structure deems to be expanded, enhancing the reliability of data processing. Therefore, the BLS is considered as a promising tool for QoE modeling and prediction.

Considering the characteristics of the BLS and the demand of QoE modeling and prediction, we propose the BLS-based multimedia QoE evaluation model, shown in Fig. 4.9.

From this figure we can see, the original input data **X** is IFs and the output **Y** is user QoE. Firstly, we divide the **X** into two parts, the objective IFs such as network parameters and content parameters, the subjective IFs such as user type, user interest, and user behavior. For the objective IFs, they are firstly mapped to feature nodes $\mathbf{Z}_1, \ldots, \mathbf{Z}_j$. Different from the original BLS, here we adopt the restricted Boltzmann machines (RBM) [13] for modeling the relationship of $\mathbf{X}_{network}$ & $\mathbf{X}_{content}$ and $\mathbf{Z}_1, \ldots, \mathbf{Z}_j$. For the subjective IFs, as its abstract properties, we directly take them as features, $\mathbf{Z}_{j+1}, \ldots, \mathbf{Z}_n$. Then, the feature nodes **Z** are mapped to enhancement nodes **H**. The relationship of **Z** and **H** is also modeled by the RBM. The reasons why the selection of RBM is that it can obtain not only the optimal mapping weights $\mathbf{W}_{in-fea}$ and $\mathbf{W}_{fea-enh}$ in an unsupervised manner, but also the associated implicit $\mathbf{Z}_1, \ldots, \mathbf{Z}_j$ and **H**, when compared with the random mapping in original BLS. After **Z** and **H** are derived, the training of **W** is identical to the original BLS. The main steps of the modeling and prediction of the proposed BLS-based multimedia QoE model are summarized in the following:

**Step 1**: Take $\mathbf{X}_{network}$ & $\mathbf{X}_{content}$ as input data, perform the contrast divergence algorithm [9] to obtain the $\mathbf{W}_{in-fea}$ and $\mathbf{Z}_1, \ldots, \mathbf{Z}_j$.

**Step 2**: Take subjective IFs related to users $\mathbf{X}_{users}$ as features $\mathbf{Z}_{j+1}, \ldots, \mathbf{Z}_n$. Therefore, feature nodes are $\mathbf{Z} = \{\mathbf{Z}_1, \ldots, \mathbf{Z}_j, \mathbf{Z}_{j+1}, \ldots, \mathbf{Z}_n\}$.

**Step 3**: Perform the contrast divergence algorithm [6] to obtain $\mathbf{W}_{fea-enh}$ and $\mathbf{H} = \{\mathbf{H}_1, \ldots, \mathbf{H}_m\}$.

**Step 4**: Combine $\mathbf{Z}$ with $\mathbf{H}$, $[\mathbf{Z}|\mathbf{H}]$. Linear mapping is used to establish the relationship between $[\mathbf{Z}|\mathbf{H}]$ and $\mathbf{Y}$. That is, $\mathbf{Y} = [\mathbf{Z}|\mathbf{H}]\mathbf{W}$, where $\mathbf{W}$ is the connecting weights for the broad structure.

**Step 5**: Estimate $\mathbf{W}$ by $\mathbf{W} = [\mathbf{Z}|\mathbf{H}]^+\mathbf{Y}$. $\mathbf{W}$ can be easily computed through the ridge regression approximation of $[\mathbf{Z}^n|\mathbf{H}^m]^+$ by using

$$[\mathbf{Z}^n|\mathbf{H}^m]^+ = \lim_{\lambda \to 0} (\lambda I + [\mathbf{Z}^n|\mathbf{H}^m] \cdot [\mathbf{Z}^n|\mathbf{H}^m]^{\mathrm{T}})^{-1} \cdot [\mathbf{Z}^n|\mathbf{H}^m]^{\mathrm{T}}. \quad (4.22)$$

It is noted that all of the incremental learning algorithms in [8] are effective here.

**Step 6**: After training is finished, QoE can be predicted for new coming data by the established model.

For testing the performance of the BLS-based QoE modeling and prediction, experimental results are implemented, which will directly determine the final management of QoE. In order to evaluate the performance of the BLS, we also select two competing schemes: deep learning network (DLN) and decision tree (DT). Specifically, BLS, DLN, and DT are, respectively, implemented in the Spark platform to obtain the QoE level. In Fig. 4.10, we compare QoE distribution in the proposed architecture with those based on DT and DLN. From this figure we can see, 90% of users obtain QoE higher than 3 for BLS and DLN. Furthermore, when

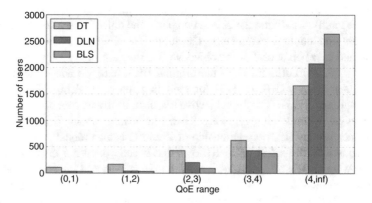

**Fig. 4.10** Performance comparison of DT, DLN, and BLS in terms of QoE distribution

concerning the proportions of users whose QoE are higher than 4, the performance of BLS is superior to those of DLN and DT. Moreover, we also compare training time of the DT, DLN, and BLS, which are 390.87 s, 45,143.43 s, and 63.21 s. We can see that the training time of the BLS has been substantially reduced compared with the deep learning model.

## 4.4 Summary

In this chapter, our works about multimedia QoE modeling and prediction have been described. Firstly, two multimedia user complaint modeling and prediction algorithms based on imbalanced data processing are investigated. Subsequently, multimedia QoE modeling and prediction based on ANN and LSTM-Attention network are discussed. Finally, a BLS-based multimedia QoE modeling and prediction is proposed.

## References

1. He H, Garcia EA (2009) Learning from imbalanced data. IEEE Trans Knowl Data Eng 21(9):3126–1284
2. Wei X, Li C, Zhou L, Zhao L (2015) Distributed density estimation based on a mixture of factor analyzers in sensor network. Sensors 15(8):19047–19068
3. Wei X, Li C (2012) The infinite Student's t-mixture for robust modeling. Signal Process 92(1):224–234
4. Wei X, Li Z, Liu R, Zhou L (2017) IPTV user's complaint based on the Gaussian mixture model for imbalanced dataset. J Comput 28(6):216–224
5. Wang L, Jin J, Huang R, Wei X, Chen J (2016) Unbiased decision tree model for user's QoE in imbalanced dataset. In: International conference on cloud computing research and innovation, Singapore, May 4–5, pp 114–119
6. Rutkowski L, Jaworski M, Pietruczuk L, Duda P (2014) The CART decision tree for mining data streams. Inf Sci 266:1–15
7. Zhou Z (2016) Machine learning. Tsinghua University Press, Beijing
8. Huang R, Wei X, Gao Y, Lv C, Mao J, Bao Q (2018) Data-driven QoE prediction for IPTV service. Comput Commun 118(12):195–204
9. Goodfellow I, Bengio Y, Courville A (2016) Deep learning. The MIT Press, Cambridge
10. Vaswani A, Shazeer N, Parmar N, Uszkoreit J, Jones L, Gomez AN, Kaiser L, Polosukhin I (2017) Attention is all you need. In: Advances in neural information processing systems, Long Beach, CA, Dec 4–9, pp 1–8
11. Mao J (2019) Design and implementation of IPTV user experience prediction system on neural network. Master Thesis, Nanjing University of Posts and Telecommunications (Supervisor: Wei X)
12. Chen CLP, Liu Z (2018) Broad learning system: an effective and efficient incremental learning system without the need for deep architecture. IEEE Trans Neur Net Lear Syst 29(1):10–24
13. Hinton G (2010) A practical guide to training restricted Boltzmann machines. Momentum 9(1):926–947

# Chapter 5
# Implementation and Demonstration

**Abstract** In this chapter, we implement multimedia QoE evaluation on the big data processing platform and demonstrate evaluation results. Firstly, we give a brief introduction to the framework of big data platform. Then, we describe the realization procedure of multimedia QoE evaluation containing data collection, storage, analysis, and mining. Finally, we introduce the demonstration of multimedia QoE evaluation results.

## 5.1 Establishment of Big Data Platform

When concerning implementation of multimedia QoE evaluation, we need to establish a big data platform, which mainly includes multimedia QoE data collection, multimedia QoE data storage, multimedia QoE data analysis and mining, multimedia QoE data demonstration, shown in Fig. 5.1.

Multimedia QoE data collection refers to obtaining various types of structured, semi-structured, and unstructured massive data in network devices and terminal devices of IPTV, OTT services. Multimedia QoE data storage should store the collected data in memory, construct and manage a corresponding database. At the same time, it depends on the reliable distributed file system, energy-optimized storage, computing integration into storage, multimedia QoE data deduplication and efficient low-cost multimedia QoE data storage techniques, distributed non-relational multimedia QoE data management and processing techniques, etc. Multimedia QoE data analysis and mining are based on data collection and storage, which are implemented and verified according to the proposed training and prediction algorithms. In practical applications, distributed technique is needed to realize distributed parallel usage of computing and processing resources.

According to the functional requirements of the multimedia QoE evaluation, combined with the current popular open source data processing tools, the architecture of big data platform for multimedia QoE evaluation is proposed, shown in Fig. 5.2.

X. Wei, L. Zhou, *Multimedia QoE Evaluation*, SpringerBriefs in Computer Science,
https://doi.org/10.1007/978-3-030-23350-1_5

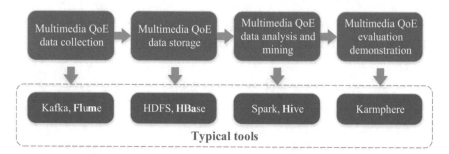

**Fig. 5.1** Flow chart of realization for multimedia QoE evaluation

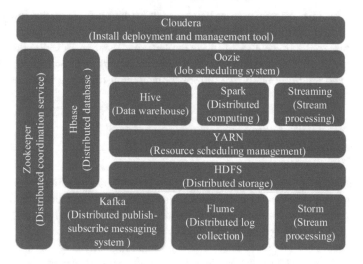

**Fig. 5.2** Architecture of big data platform for multimedia QoE evaluation

Specifically, it uses Kafka for data caching, Flume for data collection, HDFS for distributed storage system, and HBase for distributed storage database [1, 2]. Moreover, it selects Spark for distributed parallel computing framework, supplemented by Storm/Streaming as real-time stream. In the calculation, it adopts YARN to perform resource scheduling management and Zookeeper to realize distributed coordination service.

In order to automate the installation and deployment for the big data platform, and to manage various components at the same time, we firstly introduce the multimedia QoE data management tool Cloudera before describing the various components of platform.

## 5.2   Multimedia QoE Data Management Tool

As a powerful commercial data center management tool, Cloudera provides a variety of data computing frameworks that can run quickly and stably, such as Apache Spark. Users can perform Cloudera to manage and install HBase distributed column NoSQL database. Moreover, Cloudera includes the native Hadoop search engine and navigator optimizer to perform a visual coordinated optimization of the computing tasks on Hadoop to improve operation efficiency  [3, 4]. At the same time, the components provided in Cloudera enable users to easily manage, configure, and monitor Spark and all the other related components in a visual UI interface with certain fault tolerance and disaster tolerance processing. In a word, Cloudera as a widely used data center management tool provides huge guarantees for security.

At the heart of Cloudera Manager is the management server, which hosts the web server and application logic of the management console and is responsible for installing the software, configuring, starting and stopping services, and running the cluster on the management service.

### 5.2.1   Architecture of Cloudera Manager

The Cloudera Manager server consists of the following components, as shown in Fig. 5.3.

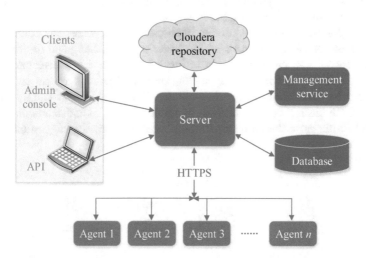

**Fig. 5.3**  Architecture of Cloudera Manager (http://www.cloudera.com/documentation/enterprise/6/6.2/topics/cm_intro_primer.html)

Agent: installed on each host. The agent is responsible for starting and stopping the process, unpacking the configuration, triggering the device, and monitoring the host.

Management service: a group of services that perform various monitoring, alerting, and reporting functions.

Database: store configurations and monitor information. Typically, multiple logical databases run on one or more database servers. For example, Cloudera's management server and monitoring roles use different logical databases.

Cloudera repository: the software manages distributed repositories by Cloudera.

Clients: the interface used to interact with the server.

Admin console: web-based user interface with administrator management cluster and Cloudera management.

API: for creating custom Cloudera Manager applications with developers.

### 5.2.2   Cluster and Service Management

Based on the powerful Cloudera Manager management tool, installation and deployment processes are no longer described for all components in the established multimedia QoE data platform.

In the design of multimedia QoE data analysis subsystem, combined with the hardware facilities of the laboratory and the multimedia QoE evaluation requirements, a high-performance computing cluster consisting of 39 computing nodes and 2 management nodes is established, shown in Fig. 5.4. One of the two management nodes is a master node and the other is a backup node.

Here, Cloudera Manager is used to implement cluster management and service management. Node management in the cluster such as adding and deleting nodes can be handled conveniently, shown in Fig. 5.5. The service management shown in Fig. 5.6 directly realizes the appending and configuration of the components integrated by Cloudera Manager. In addition, Cloudera Manager can monitor the health of the cluster, comprehensively monitor the various indicators and system operations, diagnose the problems in the cluster, and provide suggestions for the problems.

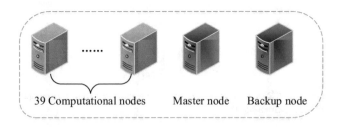

**Fig. 5.4** Cluster composition of our big data platform for multimedia QoE evaluation

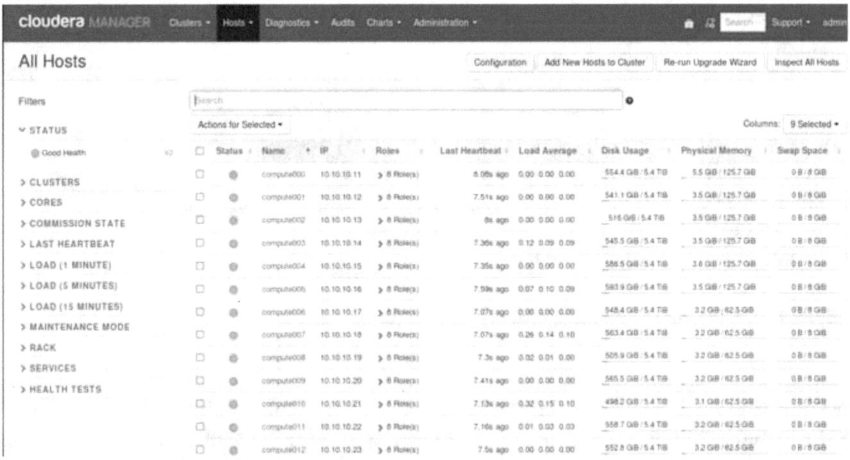

**Fig. 5.5**  Interface of node management in the cluster

**Fig. 5.6**  Interface of service management

## 5.3  Multimedia QoE Data Collection and Storage

### 5.3.1  Multimedia QoE Data Collection

Flume is a distributed, reliable, and highly available log collection system for massive log collection, aggregation, and transmission. It supports the customization of various data senders in the log system for data collection. At the same time, Flume provides the ability to simply process data and write to various data recipients. Kafka is a distributed, partitionable, replicable messaging system that maintains message queues.

In the architecture of the multimedia QoE data collection subsystem shown in Fig. 5.7, Kafka uses producer API to publish messages to one or more topics. It

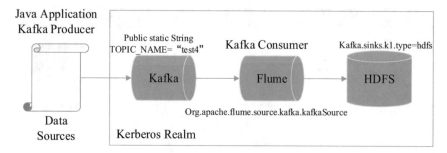

**Fig. 5.7** Architecture of multimedia QoE data collection subsystem

uses streams API as a stream processor to consume input streams from one or more topics, and generate an output stream to one or more topics, effectively converting the input stream to the output stream. Moreover, it uses consumer API to subscribe to one or more topics and process the resulting message.

The procedure of multimedia QoE data collection is described as follows:

**Step 1**:   Enable and configure Kerberos in Kafka cluster
            Log into Cloudera Manager and enter Kafka service. Modify *Kerberos.auth.enable* and *security.inter.broker.protocol* to enable Kerberos authentication and save the configuration.

**Step 2**:   Configure the Kafka cluster environment and start Kafka

(1) Generate a keytab file for accessing the Kafka cluster. Execute the following command on the Kerberos service. It can be seen that the keytab file of the fayson@CLOUDERA.COM account is generated in the current directory.

```
[root@node000 kafkatest]# pwd /opt/kafkatest
[root@node000kafkatest]# kadmin.local
Authenticating as principal
hdfs/admin@CLOUDERA.COM with password.
kadmin.local: xst−norandkey
            −k fayson.keytab fayson@CLOUDERA.COM
```

(2) Create a jaas.conf file.

```
KafkaClient {
com.sun.security.auth.module.Krb5LoginModule required
useKeyTab=true
keyTab=''/keytab/fayson.keytab''
principal=''fayson@CLOUDERA.COM'';
};
```

(3) Copy the keytab file and jaas.conf file to all nodes running by Flume agent.
            Here we copy the above configuration file in the "flume-keytab" directory of the Flume agent.

(4) Modify the directory file owner to ensure that Flume user has permission to access.

```
[bigdata@node000 kafkatest flume−keytab]$ sudo chown −R
                                      flume. /flume−keytab/
[bigdata@node000 kafkatest flume−keytab]$ sudo chmod −R
                                      755/flume−keytab/
```

(5) Start Zookeeper.

```
[root@node000 zookeeper]# zkServer.sh start
```

(6) Start Kafka.

```
[root@node000 kafkatest]# kafka−server−start.sh config
                          /server.properties &
```

(7) Create Kafka topic.

```
[root@node000 kafkatest]# kafka−topics.sh—create —
                          zookeeper s201:2181−−replication
                          —factor 3—partitions 3—topic
                          itemtest
```

(8) Start consumption topic.

```
[root@node000 kafkatest]# kafka−console−consumer.sh—
              bootstrap−server s201:9092,s202:9092,s203:9092
              —zookeepers201:2181,s202:2181,s203:2181−−topic
              mytest—from−beginning
```

**Step 3**:   Configure Flume agent

(1) Configure Flume agent to read Kafka data and write it to HDFS.

```
kafka.channels = c1
kafka.sources = s1
kafka.sinks = k1
kafka.sources.s1.type =org.apache.flume.source.
                      kafka.KafkaSource
kafka.sources.s1.kafka.bootstrap.servers =ip−172−31−26
              −80.ap−southeast−1.compute.internal:9092,
              ip−172−31−21−45.ap−southeast−1.compute.
              9092,ip−172−31−26−102.ap−southeast
              internal:−1.compute.internal:9092
kafka.sources.s1.kafka.topics = test4
kafka.sources.s1.kafka.consumer.group.id = flume−consumer
kafka.sources.s1.kafka.consumer.security.protocol
                              = SASL_PLAINTEXT
kafka.sources.s1.kafka.consumer.sasl.mechanism = GSSAPI
kafka.sources.s1.kafka.consumer.sasl.kerberos.service.
                              name = kafka
kafka.sources.s1.channels = c1
kafka.channels.c1.type = memory
kafka.sinks.k1.type = hdfs
kafka.sinks.k1.channel = c1
```

```
kafka . sinks . k1 . hdfs . kerberosKeytab  =  /flume−keytab/
                                               fayson . keytab
kafka . sinks . k1 . hdfs . kerberosPrincipal=fayson@CLOUDERA .COM
kafka . sinks . k1 . hdfs . path  =  /tmp/kafka−test
kafka . sinks . k1 . hdfs . filePrefix  =  events−
kafka . sinks . k1 . hdfs . writeFormat  =  Text
```

(2)  Increase the Flume agent startup parameters.

```
−Djava . security . auth . login . config =/flume−keytab/jaas . conf
```

(3)  Save and start the Flume agent service after finishing configuration.

```
[ root@node000  flume ]#  flume−ng agent −n producer −c conf
                         −f flume−kafka−sink . properties
                         −Dflume . root . logger  =  ERROR, console
```

**Step 4**:    Adopt Java Message Service
It is a typical implementation of message data transmission, which can
take synchronous, asynchronous, and reliable message processing.

(1)  Write the jaas.conf file to complete the java access Kerberos settings
in Kafka.

```
KafkaClient {
    com . sun . security . auth . module . Krb5LoginModule  required
    useKeyTab  =  true
    keyTab  =  ''/opt/run−kafka/conf/fayson . keytab ''
    principal  =  ''fayson@CLOUDERA .COM' ';
};
```

(2)  Write message production code in Java.
(3)  Compile, package, and export the java production code.

```
mvn  clean  package
mvn  dependency : copy−dependencies  −DoutputDirectory
                                   =  /opt/fayson/lib
```

(4)  In order to run the test jar package, write "run.sh" script.

```
#!/bin/bash
JAVA_HOME=/usr/java/jdk1 .8.0 _131−cloudera
for  file  in  'ls  lib/*jar '
do
        CLASSPATH=$CLASSPATH: $file
done
export  CLASSPATH
${JAVA_HOME}/bin/java com . cloudera . ProducerTest
```

(5)  Confirm the conf configuration file in the Kafka directory.

```
Fayson . keytab : fayson 's keytab file
Jaas . conf : java access
              configuration in Kerberos environment
Krb5 . conf : cluster krb5 configuration file
```

**Step 5**: Perform Kafka⟶Flume⟶HDFS process test

(1) Execute the "run.sh" script.

```
[ root@node000 run−kafka ]# sh run . sh
```

(2) View the Kafka log and view the running information.

```
[ root@node000 logs ]# cat kafka . log
```

(3) View the data in the HDFS directory.

```
[ root@node000 /]# hadoop fs −ls / QoEfile / data
[ root@node000 /]# hadoop fs −text / QoEfile / data / events
                  −1314034355162
```

### 5.3.2 Multimedia QoE Data Storage

Hadoop distribute file system (HDFS) and HBase are adopted to realize multimedia QoE data storage.

HDFS is a Hadoop distributed file system that allows large-scale, highly fault-tolerant distributed, and parallel computing clusters to be built on multiple nodes in a Hadoop cluster, providing high-performance and high-throughput data access as well as large amounts of data storage. Figure 5.8 shows the file read and write operation flow in HDFS. There is only one NameNode, which is responsible for accepting user requests, maintaining the relationships among file system, management files, Blocks, and DataNodes. In the HDFS architecture, there are multiple DataNodes responsible for data storage. The DataNode divides the data

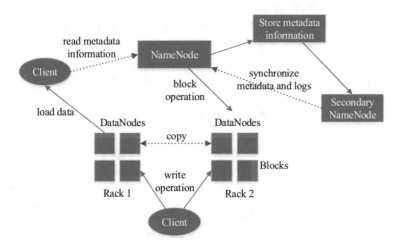

**Fig. 5.8** Flowchart for reading and writing files in HDFS [5]

**Fig. 5.9** Four-dimensional
data model in HBase [5]

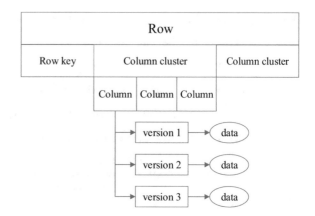

into multiple Blocks and stores them on the disk, and also backs up the data to
ensure data security.

HBase is a distributed, non-relational open source database [6]. It is also a
high reliability, high performance, column oriented, scalable distributed storage
system. Similar to HDFS, HBase can also implement large-scale structured storage
on common servers, saving system construction costs. HBase is an important part
of the Apache Hadoop ecosystem. It is a distributed database built on HDFS and is
mainly used for storing massive data.

HBase uses a four-dimensional data model to define the data as shown in Fig. 5.9.
A row key is an identifier that is owned by each row of data in a table. It is a
byte array with no data type. Each column in the table must belong to a certain
column cluster. Since HBase will save the column cluster to its own data file total,
the column cluster needs to be defined in advance and cannot be modified at will.
With the definition in the relational database, the column represents the real column
of data, but each column in HBase has a version number. When accessing the data,
the data of the column can be obtained by the version at different times.

## 5.4  Multimedia QoE Data Analysis and Mining

### 5.4.1  Operating Principle of Spark

Apache Spark is a fast and versatile computing engine designed for big data
processing. It is a big data distributed computing framework based on in-memory
computing. Based on memory computing, Spark improves the real-time performance of data processing while ensuring high fault tolerance and high scalability
[7]. It allows users to deploy Spark on a large number of inexpensive hardware
to form a cluster. In a Spark cluster, a master node is responsible for central
coordination called a driver node, and the corresponding worker node is called an
executor node, shown in Fig. 5.10. The driver and all nodes are collectively referred

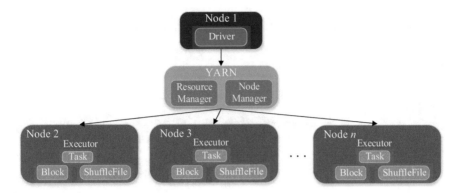

**Fig. 5.10** Running process of Spark on YARN

to as a Spark application. Just like the QoE prediction model program in IPTV, it is also used by the driver to coordinate the resource manager and the node manager through Yarn, and then schedule each distributed working node, so that the actuator can process it.

## 5.4.2  Data Analysis and Mining by Spark

(1)  Create a Spark application

**Step 1**:  Determine the development tools and language.
Here, IntelliJ IDEA and Spark-shell are used. IntelliJ IDEA is the integrated environment for developing, while Spark-shell is interactive analysis for code. The underlying scripting language of Spark is Scala.

**Step 2**:  Build a SBT-based Scala project, configure the version of Scala, add dependencies for the program, and add Spark dependencies.

```
name : = ''test''
version : = ''0.1''
scalaVersion : = ''2.11.11''
libraryDependencies + = ''org.apache.spark'' %
                ''spark−core_2.11'' % ''2.2.0''
libraryDependencies + = ''org.apache.spark'' %
                ''spark−sql_2.11'' % ''2.2.0''
libraryDependencies + = ''org.apache.spark'' %
                ''spark−mllib_2.11'' % ''2.2.0''
libraryDependencies + = ''org.apache.spark'' %
                ''spark−streaming_2.11'' % ''2.2.0''
libraryDependencies + = ''org.apache.spark'' %
                ''spark−graphx_2.11'' % ''2.2.0''
```

**Fig. 5.11** Spark-job monitoring port

**Step 3**:    Combine Spark-shell with IntelliJ IDEA to write multimedia QoE data
          analysis code.

(2)  Test multimedia QoE data analysis code

**Step 1**:    Compile and package the built Scala project and determine the main
          function of the program.

**Step 2**:    Submit the compiled jar package using Spark-submit.

> spark2−submit —class QoEModel —master yarn —deploy
> −mode cluster /home/process.jar

**Step 3**:    Check the running status of the spark program.
          As shown in Fig. 5.11, the compiled jar is uploaded to the Spark cluster
          through spark2-submit, and the execution status of the corresponding job
          is generated. Figure 5.12 shows the running status of the task in the
          submitted jar package. The job is composed of multiple stages, while each
          stage consists of multiple tasks.

(3)  Performance optimization

The details of job, stage, and task can be seen in Figs. 5.11 and 5.12. However,
how to allocate existing computing resources to achieve efficient execution of the
program is important. When the spark-submit submits the jar package, it can directly
optimize the parameters to effectively utilize the effective resources. Optimization
is handled from three perspectives.

(i)  Optimization of operating environment

In the process of compiling and packaging, if unnecessary dependencies are
added, the memory occupied by the jar package will be directly increased, and the
waste of resources caused by uploading and distributing the jar package is increased.

The data storage format will directly affect the size of the data. It can also reduce
the memory occupied by the data.

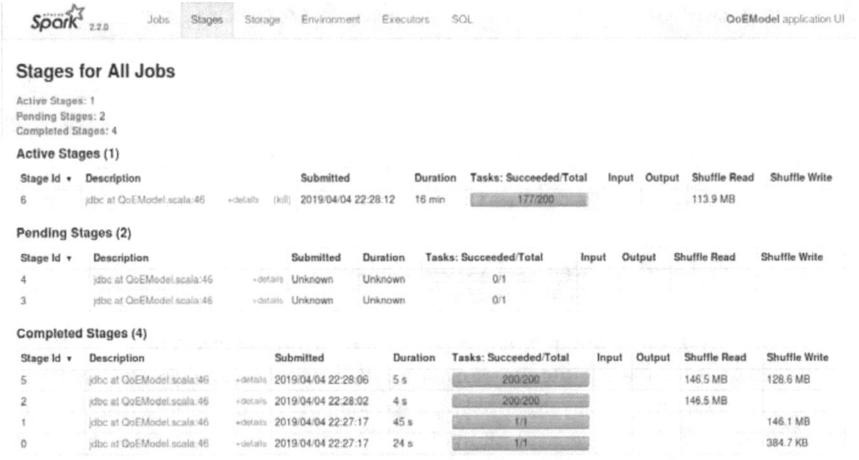

**Fig. 5.12** The running state of the stage in the Spark application

(ii) Optimization of operators in code

In the Spark application, some operators generate huge overhead that affects the efficiency of the code. In multimedia QoE data processing, you should avoid using the shuffle operation and replace it with operations such as coalesce or reparation.

Choose a reasonable partition key and set "spark.speculation" to true to avoid skew or task skew when processing data. In addition, since a Spark application consists of multiple jobs, if there are no dependencies between jobs, parallelization can be done to make full use of resources.

(iii) Fine tuning of parameter in submitted jobs

The first is to use the appropriate amount of resources, the memory size of the driver, the number of executors, the memory size of the executor, and an executor can process the number of tasks in parallel. The number of hardware resources used can be passed through driver-memory, executor-memory, executor-cores to set.

The second is to set reasonable JVM parameters:

```
spark . driver . extraJavaOptions ,
spark . executor . extraJavaOptions ,
−conf  spark . executor . extraJavaOptions
−''−XX:+UseConcMarkSweepGC
    −XX: Permsize =64m
    −XX: MaxPermSize  =256m''
```

After giving some more common tuning parameter configurations, it needs to use them in combination with specific situations.

## 5.5    Multimedia QoE Evaluation Result Demonstration

After performing the multimedia QoE evaluation techniques to the big data plat-form, the last procedure is to demonstrate the evaluation results. In this section, we briefly show our developed interface for demonstration by ECharts [8].

### 5.5.1    User Complaint Prediction Result

Firstly, we perform user complaint prediction demonstration based on IPTV service dataset. In order to deepen the understanding of the user's viewing data, under the data analysis module, the system displays the statistics and analysis results of the data. Figure 5.13 shows the total number of IPTV users, the number of IPTV user complaints, and the distribution of user complaints. The system focuses on the monthly distribution of complaints from IPTV users and the TOP5 cities for user complaints.

### 5.5.2    User Interest Inference Result

User viewing behavior can reflect user viewing interest. Therefore, according to the user viewing records, average viewing time of the user can be counted, the video program frequently viewed by the user can be collected, and the viewing behavior information of the user can be extracted, thereby analyzing the viewing interest of the user. The user viewing interest interface mainly includes the user viewing time, shown in Fig. 5.14, and the user viewing program information, shown in Fig. 5.15. Among them, user viewing time is based on data preprocessing and analysis, reflecting the user daily viewing habit within 1 month. Statistics are performed on the program channels viewed by users in the dataset, and ten channels with the

**Fig. 5.13**  User complaint prediction results

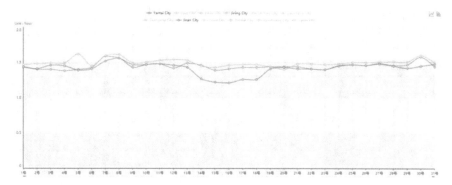

**Fig. 5.14** User daily viewing time

**Fig. 5.15** Top10 program cloud

most views in a month are obtained, forming a Top10 character cloud of the video interface.

### 5.5.3   User QoE Prediction Result

Here, user QoE is the subjective feeling after watching video programs, that is, the degree of satisfaction with the multimedia service. Demonstration of multimedia QoE prediction is the core function of the system, containing the following two main interface:

1. Accuracy of QoE prediction for different models is shown in Fig. 5.16.
2. Changes of user QoE in a certain period of time are displayed in Fig. 5.17.

   Using the above interface, multimedia service content providers and network operators can conveniently monitor and check the dynamic of QoE, so as to take actions to improve service quality and promote user feeling. It is noted that the above system has been successfully used by two operators in China.

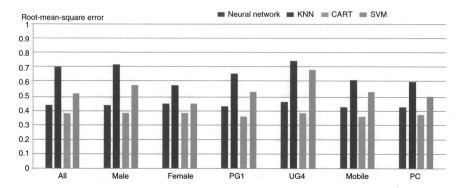

**Fig. 5.16** Accuracy of QoE prediction for different models

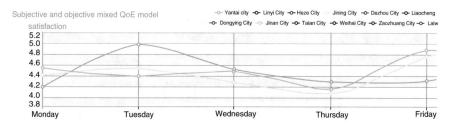

**Fig. 5.17** Changes of user QoE in a certain period of time

## 5.6   Summary

In this chapter, a big data platform for implementation and demonstration of multimedia QoE evaluation is presented and described. In order to clearly collect and store multimedia service data, we firstly describe multimedia QoE data collection and storage. Subsequently, we give the realization of multimedia QoE data analysis and mining. Finally, we develop related interfaces to demonstrate the multimedia QoE evaluation results.

## References

1. Noac HL, Costan A, Bouge L (2017) A performance evaluation of Apache Kafka in support of big data streaming applications. In: IEEE international conference on big data, Boston, MA, Dec 11–14, pp 4803–4806
2. Khan M, Jin Y, Li M, Xiang Y, Jiang C (2016) Hadoop performance modeling for job estimation and resource provisioning. IEEE Trans Parallel Distrib Syst 27(2):441–454
3. Cheng D, Zhou X, Lama P, Ji M, Jiang C (2018) Energy efficiency aware task assignment with DVFS in heterogeneous hadoop clusters. IEEE Trans Parallel Distrib Syst 29(1):70–82
4. Malik M, Neshatpour K, Rafatirad S, Homayoun H (2018) Hadoop workloads characterization for performance and energy efficiency optimizations on microservers. IEEE Trans Multiscale Comput Syst 4(3):355–368

5. Liu Q (2017) Design and implementation of IPTV fault location system in big data environment. Master Thesis, Nanjing University of Posts and Telecommunications (Supervisor: Zhou L)
6. Dede E, Sendir B, Kuzlu P, Weachock J, Govindaraju M, Ramakrishnan L (2016) Processing Cassandra datasets with Hadoop-streaming based approaches. IEEE Trans Serv Comput 9(1):46–58
7. Ramirez-Gallego S, Mourino-Talin H, Martinez-Rego D, Bolon-Canedo V, Benitez JM, Alonso-Betanzos A, Herrera F (2018) An information theory-based feature selection framework for big data under Apache Spark. IEEE Trans Syst Man Cybern 48(9):1441–1453
8. Bond GW, Goguen H (2002) ECharts: balancing design and implementation. In: Proceedings of the 6th IASTED international conference on software engineering and applications, Nov 4–6, pp 149–155

# Chapter 6
# Conclusion

**Abstract** In this chapter, we summarize the main innovations and contributions of this book before future work is discussed.

## 6.1  Concluding Remarks

With the development of information technology, future multimedia service emphasizes not only speed, bandwidth, quality of service sources, but also user feeling and satisfaction. By considering the demand of QoE perception and monitoring from content providers and network operators, we aim to introduce several works about multimedia QoE evaluation by our research group in this book. The main innovations and contributions include:

1. We describe three representative datasets obtained in our research. One is from a network operator and the others are collected and crawled by ourselves. Moreover, considering the importance of abstract and subjective user-related IFs for multimedia QoE, we give data preprocessing and feature extraction algorithms for five user-related IFs, namely user viewing time ratio, user interest, user type, user behavior, and comment & danmaku.
2. Based on the extracted features, we introduce several of our proposed models and prediction algorithms for multimedia QoE evaluation. Firstly, considering the existence of imbalance dataset in multimedia user complaint prediction, we propose the GMM-based oversampling algorithm and the decision tree-based cost-sensitive algorithm. Subsequently, we perform two neural networks, ANN and LSTM-Attention network to predict multimedia QoE. Finally, considering the real-time demand in current applications, we design the BLS-based modeling and prediction algorithm.
3. Based on the theoretical research results, we design and realize multimedia QoE evaluation by a big data platform. Firstly, in order to clearly collect and store multimedia service data, we design data collection and storage strategies. Then, we implement data analysis and mining by taking advantage of Spark. Finally,

X. Wei, L. Zhou, *Multimedia QoE Evaluation*, SpringerBriefs in Computer Science,
https://doi.org/10.1007/978-3-030-23350-1_6

we show the evaluation results in the big data platform by developing related interfaces by ECharts.

## 6.2   Future Work

Multimedia QoE evaluation is a promising research topic now, which is also greatly significant for multimedia information processing. This book provides guidance on how to perform multimedia QoE evaluation in the era of big data. Further research work should be concerned in the future studies including:

1. Currently, most multimedia QoE evaluation research works do not take into account the time series characteristics of the user experience. For example, when a user is watching at home, QoE may not be changed obviously. On the contrary, if he/she is watching in a train, QoE may fluctuate sharply. Therefore, temporal correlations are needed to be considered when designing multimedia QoE modeling and prediction algorithm. In other words, future researches should consider the changing factors of user experience over time and the evaluation of user experience and impact factors in real-time situations.
2. After multimedia QoE is evaluated, how to take effective actions to continuously promote QoE is also an important and valuable research direction. Specifically, QoE is influenced by various objective and subjective factors. Therefore, besides the evaluated QoE, crucial factors influencing QoE should also be accurately determined. Moreover, due to the dynamic characteristics of QoE, how to automatically alter the crucial IFs to guarantee QoE in a high level is significative. As deep reinforcement learning can automatically track the objects and take actions, we think it is a promising tool for handling this issue.

Printed in the United States
By Bookmasters